structuring your NOVEL WORKBOOK

Hands-On Help for Building Strong and Successful Stories

structuring your NOVEL WORKBOOK

Hands-On Help for Building Strong and Successful Stories

K.M. WEILAND

SCOTTSBLUFF, NEBRASKA

Dedicated to my beloved Savior, who uses life to teach me about story and stories to teach me about life.

And to Becca Puglisi, who is one of the kindest, most generous, and all-around loveliest people with whom I've been privileged to share the writing road.

Also by K.M. Weiland:

Outlining Your Novel: Map Your Way to Success

Outlining Your Novel Workbook: Step-by-Step Exercises for Planning Your Best Book

Structuring Your Novel: Essential Keys for Writing an Outstanding Story

Jane Eyre: The Writer's Digest Annotated Classic

Conquering Writer's Block and Summoning Inspiration

Fiction
A Man Called Outlaw

Behold the Dawn

Dreamlander

Digital Shorts
The Memory Lights

One More Ride in the Rain

The Saddle Daddy Rode

TABLE OF CONTENTS

INTRODUCTION

ONE THING I always stress to writers is the importance of writing subjects you're passionate about. Most of the time, this advice is aimed at novelists, but it applies equally when I'm writing non-fiction how-to books like *Structuring Your Novel: Essential Keys for Writing an Outstanding Story*—on which this workbook is based. In fact, when it comes to structure, "passionate" may be too small a word to describe my feelings.

The concept of story structure has led me to some of the greatest discoveries and epiphanies in my journey as a writer. Even today, I can't begin to describe how excited I continue to be by the whole idea.

Once you understand the common elements in all good stories, a veil lifts from your eyes. You've always seen the stories; you've even understood them to some extent. But suddenly you're viewing story from a whole new dimension. It's like an X-ray machine. Where once you only saw the surface skin and hair, now you get to see the story skeleton.

Like most authors, I've done my share of battling with recalcitrant first drafts. Even with a solid outline, some stories just didn't want to cooperate, and I would spill my quart of blood and pound of flesh, working my heart out to make them better. Many of us think that's the only way.

But it doesn't have to be.

WHY STRUCTURE WILL MAKE YOUR WRITING BETTER AND EASIER

Too often, writers get hung up on the idea that writing is supposed to be this airy-fairy, instinctive feeling that *flows* out of us. We mess with that, and, pfft, forget artistic genius. Like so many writers, I spent my early years in the craft struggling along, pounding out my brains against my keyboard, writing stories that *almost* worked, but that just weren't quite there.

Back then, I liked to compare writing to digging myself out of a hole. I didn't know what was in the hole. I didn't even know what the next shovelful was supposed to look like. I just kept digging, trusting I would eventually reach the bottom, where it would all make sense.

This is how many of us write. We know there's a checklist of "story must-haves" necessary to make the story work. As long as we've incorporated a strong hook in the beginning, characters with pronounced arcs, and rising suspense, then we're supposed to be able to reach the end of the story (the bottom of the hole) where everything will suddenly fall into place.

But you've probably written at least one story that didn't work out quite that way. You did everything right (as far as you knew), and yet the story still bombed. *And you had no idea why.* Talk about frustrating. You checked all the "must-have" elements off your list just like you were supposed to. But something went wrong. Those elements just didn't hang together the way they were supposed to.

That is where structure comes into play.

The first time I heard structure explained to me, point by point, a light bulb practically exploded in my head. I was ready to get up and jump on the bed and turn somersaults and kiss the cat. It, quite literally, changed my life.

In my book *Structuring Your Novel*, I have broken the basic principles of the three-act structure into a fundamentally simple approach. Piece by piece, the book examines each important element in your story: the Hook, the First Act, the First Plot Point, the First Half of the Second Act, the Midpoint, the Second Half of the Second Act, the Third Plot Point, the Third Act, the Climax, and the Resolution. More than that, it also discusses the smaller building blocks of the story—particularly the intricacies of scene structure.

HOW TO USE THIS WORKBOOK

In this workbook, you will discover all of these principles, via step-by-step guides for crafting each important structural element and specific questions for narrowing your focus. If you're an outliner, you can use this workbook to help you plan a structurally sound story before you ever begin your first draft (the methods discussed here work hand in hand with those I teach in *Outlining Your Novel* and the *Outlining Your Novel Workbook*). You can also use this workbook to analyze an already completed manuscript, confirm its structural strengths, and identify its weaknesses.

Each chapter offers an introduction to the concepts discussed in the exercises, as well as examples from popular books and movies. I have also included a page-number guide to help you locate the associated chapters in *Structuring Your Novel*. I recommend you start by reading that book—just as you would a textbook—before embarking on the workbook. You will understand the principles and their applicability better in context.

Each chapter of the workbook builds upon the next, in a series of steps that will help you move from your story's big picture to the smaller details and back again. The more thorough you are in responding to each question and filling in each blank, the more prepared you will be to write or revise your novel. But don't hesitate to skip around. Some of the sections (such as those on foreshadowing) can't be completed until you've finished all the other steps.

Your answers may require more space than what is provided in these pages. Before you begin the exercises, grab a notebook so you can migrate your note-taking should you need more space.

The beauty of story structure is that it's ridiculously simple. Once you visualize your story as made up of these precise building blocks, you will suddenly be able to understand what makes stories work. You won't feel blind anymore. You will be able to approach your story from a place of knowledge and empowerment.

From now on, you get to be the master of your story, instead of its slave.

PART 1
STRUCTURING YOUR STORY

1
THE HOOK

WHERE DOES IT BELONG?

1% OF THE WAY INTO YOUR STORY.

OUR DISCUSSION OF story structure very naturally begins at the beginning—and every good story begins with a hook. If you fail to hook readers into your story from the very first chapter, they won't swim in deep enough to experience the rest of your rousing adventure, no matter how amazing it is.

The hook comes in many forms, but stripped to the lowest common denominator, it's nothing more or less than a question. If you can pique your readers' curiosity, you've got 'em. Simple as that.

The beginning of every story should present character, setting, and conflict. But, in themselves, none of these represents a hook. You've created a hook only when you've convinced readers to ask the general question, "What's going to happen?" because you've first convinced them to ask a very specific question.

THE HOOK QUESTION

YOUR OPENING QUESTION might be explicit: perhaps the protagonist is wondering something, which will, in turn, make readers wonder the same thing. But more often, the question will be implicit.

The important thing to remember about presenting this opening question is that it cannot be vague. Readers have to understand enough about the situation to mentally form a specific question. *What the heck is going on here?* does not qualify as a good opening question.

It's not necessary for the question to remain unanswered all the way to the end of the story. It's perfectly all right to answer the question in the very next paragraph, as long as you introduce another question, and another and another, to give readers a reason to keep turning those pages in search of answers.

Respond to the following questions to help you identify and refine your story's hook.

(For more information about the hook question, see pages 9-10 in *Structuring Your Novel*.)

What specific question will hook readers in your beginning? _____

_____.

EXAMPLES:

- **What scary reptilian monster killed the worker?**
  (*Jurassic Park* by Michael Crichton)

- **How does a city hunt?**
  (*Mortal Engines* by Philip Reeve)

- **Who is the one child who will never grow up?**
  (*Peter Pan* by J.M. Barrie)

How might you write this question explicitly? _____

_____.

Examples:

- "Where now? Who now? When now?"
  (*The Unnamable* by Samuel Beckett)

- "Now that I've found the way to fly, which direction should I go into the night?"
  (*Matched* by Ally Condie)

- "This is really Earth?"
  (*Angels at the Table* by Debbie Macomber)

How might you write this question implicitly? _____

_____ .

Examples:

- "I am an invisible man."
  (*Invisible Man* by Ralph Ellison)
  Implicit Question: *How is that possible—and why?*

- "Through the fence, between the curling flower spaces, I could see them hitting."
  (*The Sound and the Fury* by William Faulkner)
  Implicit Question: *Who is hitting what—and why?*

- "There was a boy called Eustace Clarence Scrubb, and he almost deserved it."
  (*The Voyage of the Dawn Treader* by C.S. Lewis)
  Implicit Question: *How could anyone possibly deserve that name?*

HOOK CHECKLIST

BEGINNINGS ARE THE sales pitch for your entire story. Doesn't matter how slam-bang your finish is, doesn't matter how fresh your dialogue is, doesn't matter if your haracters are so real they tap dance their way off the pages. If your beginning doesn't fulfill all its requirements, readers won't get far enough to discover your story's hidden merits.

Although no surefire pattern exists for the perfect opening, most good beginnings share common traits. Answer the following questions to help you check off the necessary components in your hook.

(For more information on the elements of a good hook, see pages 10-18 of *Structuring Your Novel.*)

What moment is the true beginning of your story? _____

_____.

At what moment in the story could you delete everything prior to it without

confusing readers? _____

_____.

What character(s) does your opening scene introduce?

Character #1: _____.

Have you introduced him by name? ☐ Yes ☐ No

If not, why not? _____.

Identify two ways to introduce the essence of his personality or story role:

Through action: _____.

Through dialogue: _____.

Character #2: _____.

Have you introduced him by name? ☐ Yes ☐ No

If not, why not? _____.

Identify two ways to introduce the essence of his personality or story role:

Through action: _____.

Through dialogue: _____.

Character #3: _____.

Have you introduced him by name? ☐ Yes ☐ No

If not, why not? _____.

Identify two ways to introduce the essence of his personality or story role:

Through action: _____.

Through dialogue: _____.

Character #4: _____.

Have you introduced him by name? ☐ Yes ☐ No

If not, why not? _____.

Identify two ways to introduce the essence of his personality or story role:

Through action: _____.

Through dialogue: _____.

Character #5: _____.

Have you introduced him by name? ☐ Yes ☐ No

If not, why not? _____.

Identify two ways to introduce the essence of his personality or story role:

Through action: _____.

Through dialogue: _____.

In your opening scene, what does your protagonist want? _____

_____.

What is preventing him from achieving his goal? _____

_____.

What can your characters do in this scene that will keep them in motion? _____

_____.

Where does your opening scene take place? _____.

How can you offer at least a *sense* of the setting in the opening line? _____

_____.

What tone does your opening create?

- ☐ Optimism
- ☐ Pessimism
- ☐ Defeat
- ☐ Fear
- ☐ Hope
- ☐ Sadness
- ☐ Joy
- ☐ Cynicism
- ☐ Idealism
- ☐ Anger
- ☐ Awe
- ☐ Disappointment
- ☐ Remorse
- ☐ Contempt
- ☐ Aggression
- ☐ Other _____.

What specific words or images have you used to achieve this effect?

WORDS

1._____

2._____

3._____

4._____

5._____

6._____

IMAGES

1._____

2._____

3._____

4._____

5._____

6._____

First Line Checklist

THE OPENING LINE of your book is your first (and, if you don't take advantage of it, *last*) opportunity to grab your readers' attention and give them a reason to read your story. That's a gargantuan job for a single sentence. What makes good first lines work? What about them makes us want to read on?

Use the following checklist to polish your opening line.

(For more information on opening lines, see pages 12-15 of *Structuring Your Novel.*)

Write your first line: _____

_____

_____

Opening Line Checklist:

☐ Does your opening line introduce your protagonist?

☐ Does your opening line raise a question?

☐ Does your opening line introduce a sense of the setting?

☐ Does your opening line set the tone for your story?

If necessary, revise your opening line to fulfill more of the above checklist's requirements:

_____

_____

_____

_____

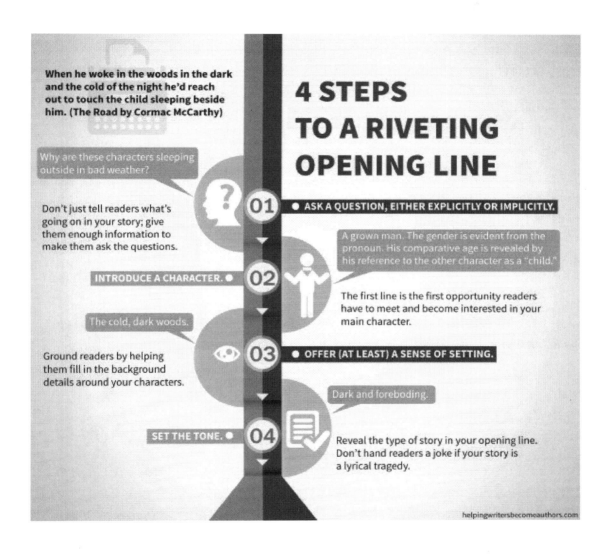

When he woke in the woods in the dark and the cold of the night he'd reach out to touch the child sleeping beside him. (The Road by Cormac McCarthy)

4 STEPS TO A RIVETING OPENING LINE

01 ● ASK A QUESTION, EITHER EXPLICITLY OR IMPLICITLY.

Why are these characters sleeping outside in bad weather?

Don't just tell readers what's going on in your story; give them enough information to make them ask the questions.

A grown man. The gender is evident from the pronoun. His comparative age is revealed by his reference to the other character as a "child."

INTRODUCE A CHARACTER. ● **02**

The first line is the first opportunity readers have to meet and become interested in your main character.

03 ● OFFER (AT LEAST) A SENSE OF SETTING.

The cold, dark woods.

Ground readers by helping them fill in the background details around your characters.

Dark and foreboding.

SET THE TONE. ● **04**

Reveal the type of story in your opening line. Don't hand readers a joke if your story is a lyrical tragedy.

helpingwritersbecomeauthors.com

THE DRAMATIC QUESTION

YOUR DRAMATIC QUESTION might be a plot question or a theme question—or both. But in order for the ending to resonate, the dramatic question must be presented in the first scene. It will always be a yes-or-no question along the lines of "Will the good guy win?" or "Will the hero learn his lesson?"

Keep in mind that *when* you choose to answer your story's main dramatic question is also important. The moment you answer this question, your story is going to be effectively over. Answer it too soon, and what's left of your plot and your character's arc will die a slow and boring death.

(For more information on the dramatic question, see pages 30-31 in *Structuring Your Novel*.)

Sum up your story's generic dramatic question: _____

_____.

EXAMPLES:

- **Will the heroine find true love?**
- **Will the antihero be redeemed?**
- **Will the bad guys suffer justice?**

Refine your story's dramatic question by filling in specific details: _____

_____.

EXAMPLES:

- **Will Margie stop her self-destructive lifestyle of drugs and liquor before she loses her soul mate Tom forever?**
- **Will mercenary Mike learn to fight for a cause more worthy than just money and power?**
- **Will the Mafia be taken down by the intrepid undercover work of FBI agent Neal?**

FORESHADOWING:

How can you foreshadow your First Plot Point in your first

chapter? _____

_____

_____.

OPENING CHAPTER CHECKLIST

I F THE MOST important thing an author can present in the beginning of any scene is a question that will hook readers into needing to know the answer, the second most important thing is making certain that question isn't the *wrong* one.

You want readers asking concrete questions. *Who stole the Statue of Liberty? How is Westley going to escape the Pit of Despair? Why did Cinderella order glass slippers a size too large?* You *don't* want them asking the dreaded four-word question: *What's going on here?* Or, worse, the end-of-the-line three-letter question: *Huh?*

Be wary of creating false suspense—the kind of suspense that has readers floundering to understand the basics of your scene—rather than forging ahead with definite and pressing questions. Supply the following answers now, so your readers won't have to.

(For more information on questions your readers shouldn't have to ask, see pages 36-38 of *Structuring Your Novel.*)

Have you introduced your characters by name? ☐ Yes ☐ No

How can you indicate your characters' general ages? _____

_____.

What important physical characteristics need to be shared to help readers form a visual image of the characters who are present in the opening scene?

1. _____

2. _____

3. _____

4. _____

5. _____

What defining facts about your characters can you supply right away?

Occupations: _____

_____.

Prominent personality traits: _____

_____.

Defining actions: _____

_____.

Other: _____

_____.

If more than one character is present, what is their relationship? _____

_____.

How can you demonstrate this to readers? _____

_____.

What setting details can you provide early on to help readers visualize your characters' surroundings?

1. _____

2. _____

3. _____

4. _____

5. _____

During what season does your story open?

☐ Spring
☐ Summer
☐ Autumn
☐ Winter

On what date does your story open?

_____ / _____ / _____

On what day of the week does your story open?
☐ S ☐ M ☐ T ☐ W ☐ T ☐ F ☐ S

If any of the specifics about the time of day at which your story opens are important, how

can you share these details with readers? _____

_____.

How can you introduce your character's goal in the first paragraph? _____

_____.

By the end of the first chapter, why will readers care enough about your story to read on?

_____

_____.

CREATIVE EXERCISE:

Think of some information readers will need to learn to understand the story. This could be technical information or character backstory. Now write an argument between two characters in which you use conflict to share this information.

SOMETHING TO THINK ABOUT:

1. Is your hook inherent to the plot?
2. Does your hook involve action (characters physically moving and/or engaging in conflict)?
3. If not, how does your hook *set up* the action?
4. Does your hook waste time before getting to the plot?
5. How does your hook pull double or triple duty in introducing character, conflict, and plot (and perhaps even setting and theme)?

RESOURCES:

- *"In Medias Res*: How to Do It and How Not to," K.M. Weiland, helping writersbecomeauthors.com/2013/09/in-medias-res
- "Character: The Most Important Part of Your Story's Beginning," K.M. Weiland, helpingwritersbecomeauthors.com/2008/05/utilizing-character-in-beginnings
- "How to Write a First Chapter That Rocks," Suzannah Windsor Freeman, helpingwritersbecomeauthors.com/SYNW-Freeman
- "8 Ways to Write a 5-Star Chapter One," Elizabeth Sims, helpingwriters becomeauthors.com/SYNW-Sims
- "Introducing Your Characters," Linda Yezak, helpingwritersbecome authors.com/SYNW-Yezak

2

THE FIRST ACT

WHERE DOES IT BELONG?

FROM THE 1% MARK TO THE 25% MARK IN YOUR STORY.

ONCE YOU'VE HOOKED readers, your next task is to put your early chapters to work introducing your characters, settings, and stakes. The first 20-25% of the book comprises your setup. At first glance, this can seem like a tremendous chunk of story to devote to introductions. But if you expect readers to stick with you throughout the story, you first have to give them a reason to care. This important stretch is where you accomplish just that. Mere curiosity can only carry readers so far. Once you've hooked that sense of curiosity, you then have to deepen the pull by creating an emotional connection between them and your characters.

These "introductions" include far more than just the actual moment of introducing the characters and settings or explaining the stakes. In themselves, the presentations of the characters probably won't take more than a few scenes. *After* the introduction is when your task of deepening the characters and establishing the stakes really begins.

FORESHADOWING

THE FIRST QUARTER of the book is the place to compile all the necessary components of your story. Anton Chekhov's famous comment that "if in the first act you have hung a pistol on the wall, then in the following one it should be fired" is just as important in reverse: if you're going to have a character fire a gun later in the book, that gun should be introduced in the First Act. The story you create in the following acts can only be assembled from the parts you've shown readers in this First Act.

Foreshadowing comes in two varieties: heavy and light.

Heavy foreshadowing plants a solid clue of what's to come later on. This kind of foreshadowing needs to happen early in the book. Your First Major Plot Point needs to be foreshadowed in your first chapter. Optimally, your Climax will also get a dab of foreshadowing early on. All the other major plot points need to be foreshadowed in the first half of the book—and preferably the first quarter.

EXAMPLES:

- In the first chapter, Ender's brutal, do-whatever-it-takes mentality in fighting off the school bully foreshadows his reactions to further bullies at the First Plot Point and Third Plot Point—and his final battle with the Formic aliens in the Climax.
(*Ender's Game* by Orson Scott Card)

- The opening line stating, "Marley was dead, to begin with.... This must be distinctly understood, or nothing wonderful can come of the story I am going to relate," foreshadows Marley's ghostly return at the First Plot Point.
(*A Christmas Carol* by Charles Dickens)

Light foreshadowing is where you remind readers of the previous heavy foreshadowing. It happens just prior to the foreshadowed event itself. This foreshadowing will almost always be applied with a much lighter touch. A little tension or foreboding or a glimpse of a symbolic motif may be all you need to poke your readers wide awake and warn them that the *something big* they've been waiting for is about to happen.

EXAMPLES:

- Ender's clash with Bonzo at the Third Plot Point is foreshadowed through tone, pacing, and the progression of Bonzo's attitude.

- Before Marley appears, Scrooge sees Marley's face in the door knocker.

A solid understanding of story structure will help you plan it to its full advantage whether you plan your foreshadowing ahead of time, allow it to emerge organically as you write, or return to reinforce it during revisions.

In the first column below, list all important characters, settings, activities, props, or events that will occur later in the story. In the second column, write ideas for foreshadowing these elements in the First Act. As you continue to fill out your structure, return to this section to note elements that should or can be foreshadowed in the first draft.

(For more information on foreshadowing in the First Act, see page 50 in *Structuring Your Novel*.)

IMPORTANT LATER IN BOOK   FORESHADOWED HOW

EXAMPLES

The Lost Boys (*Peter Pan* by J.M. Barrie)

Peter mentions them in the First Act

Little Dorrit's connection to the Clenhams (*Little Dorrit* by Charles Dickens)

The message "do not forget" in Mr. Clenham's watch

_____   _____

_____   _____

_____   _____

_____   _____

_____   _____

_____   _____

_____   _____

_____   _____

FORESHADOWING:

How can you foreshadow the Climax in the First Act? _____

_____.

SUBPLOTS

A SUBPLOT IS a thematically related exploration of a minor part of the protagonist's personality or a related aspect of theme. It's a "miniature" plot that features a sideline story. As such, subplots are vital for providing both contrast within the plot (they give readers a "break" from the main plot) and for introducing character depth via situations that would be off-limits in the main part of the plot. Most subplots will need to be introduced within the first half of the book, so they can come into full flower in the Second Act.

Consider what subplots you will introduce in the first half of your book. Write a possible subplot for each of the following categories.

(For more information on subplots, see pages 106-109 in *Structuring Your Novel*.)

Romantic Subplot: _____

_____

_____

_____.

EXAMPLE:

- **Horatio Hornblower's "accidental" marriage.**
  (*Hornblower and the Hotspur* by C.S Forester)

Career Subplot: _____

_____

_____

_____.

EXAMPLE:

- **Eva Ward's assistance at the tea house.**
  (*Rose Garden* by Susanna Kearsley)

Family Subplot: _____

_____

_____

_____.

Example:

- **Lydia and Kitty Bennet's exploits with the militia.**
  (*Pride & Prejudice* by Jane Austen)

Best Friend Subplot: _____

_____

_____

_____.

Example:

- **Harry Osborn's vendetta.**
  (*Spider-Man 2* directed by Sam Raimi)

Minor Character Arc Subplot: _____

_____

_____

_____.

Example:

- **Scrat's pursuit of the acorn.**
  (*Ice Age* directed by Chris Wedge and Carlos Saldanha)

WHICH CHARACTERS SHOULD BE INTRODUCED?

EVERY STORY WILL spread out the arrival of its important cast members in a different way. Usually, your prominent actors should all be on stage by the time the bell rings at the end of the First Act. You can find exceptions in which prominent characters don't arrive until late in the story (Aslan in C.S. Lewis's *The Lion, the Witch, and the Wardrobe*, Cynthia in Elizabeth Gaskell's *Wives and Daughters*), but these late arrivals must always be well planned. An arbitrary new character is never a good idea.

Below, identify all of your prominent characters.

(For more information on which characters should be introduced in your First Act, see pages 54-57 in *Structuring Your Novel*.)

Protagonist: _____.

Age: _____.

Occupation: _____.

Strength: _____.

Weakness: _____.

Primary Goal: _____.

How will you introduce this character? _____.

Antagonist: _____.

Age: _____.

Occupation: _____.

Strength: _____.

Weakness: _____.

Primary Goal: _____.

Connection to Protagonist: _____.

How will you introduce this character? _____.

Love interest: _____.

Age: _____.

Occupation: _____.

Strength: _____.

Weakness: _____.

Primary Goal: _____.

Connection to Protagonist: _____.

How will you introduce this character? _____.

Sidekick: _____.

Age: _____.

Occupation: _____.

Strength: _____.

Weakness: _____.

Primary Goal: _____.

Connection to Protagonist: _____.

How will you introduce this character? _____.

Mentor: _____.

Age: _____.

Occupation: _____.

Strength: _____.

Weakness: _____.

Primary Goal: _____.

Connection to Protagonist: _____.

How will you introduce this character? _____.

Other Important Character: _____.

Age: _____.

Occupation: _____.

Strength: _____.

Weakness: _____.

Primary Goal: _____.

Connection to Protagonist: _____.

How will you introduce this character? _____.

Other Important Character: _____.

Age: _____.

Occupation: _____.

Strength: _____.

Weakness: _____.

Primary Goal: _____.

Connection to Protagonist: _____.

How will you introduce this character? _____.

Other Important Character: _____.

Age: _____.

Occupation: _____.

Strength: _____.

Weakness: _____.

Primary Goal: _____.

Connection to Protagonist: _____.

How will you introduce this character? _____.

Other Important Character: _____.

Age: _____.

Occupation: _____.

Strength: _____.

Weakness: _____.

Primary Goal: _____.

Connection to Protagonist: _____.

How will you introduce this character? _____.

List all character names, nicknames, code names, etc., alphabetically. Are you overusing any one letter?

A	B	C	D
E	F	G	H
I	J	K	L
M	N	O	P
Q	R	S	T
U	V	W	X
Y	Z		

5 CHARACTERS
WHO SHOULD BE IN YOUR STORY

1 2 3 4 5

PROTAGONIST   ANTAGONIST   SIDEKICK   MENTOR   LOVE INTEREST

1 PROTAGONIST

- MAIN ACTOR.
- MOST GREATLY AFFECTED BY THE ANTAGONIST.
- REACTIONS AND ACTIONS DRIVE THE MAJORITY OF THE PLOT.
- READERS IDENTIFY WITH MOST STRONGLY.
- INNER JOURNEY MANIFESTS THEME.

2 ANTAGONIST

- DIRECTLY (VERSUS INCIDENTALLY) OPPOSED TO THE PROTAGONIST.
- PRIMARY OBSTACLE TO YOUR PROTAGONIST'S PLOT GOAL.
- SHARES IMPORTANT SIMILARITIES WITH THE PROTAGONIST.

3 SIDEKICK

- LOYAL TO AND SUPPORTIVE OF THE PROTAGONIST.
- ALIGNED WITH THE PROTAGONIST'S GOALS.
- DIFFERS FROM THE PROTAGONIST IN IMPORTANT WAYS.

4 MENTOR

- TEACHER OR HELPER TO THE PROTAGONIST
- GUARDS THE PROTAGONIST DURING HIS QUEST.
- GUIDES THE PROTAGONIST DOWN THE RIGHT PATH.
- MORAL STANDARD AGAINST WHICH THE PROTAGONIST WILL BE MEASURED.
- SUPPORTS OR OPPOSES THE PROTAGONIST, DEPENDING ON THE PROTAGONIST'S MORAL ALIGNMENT.

5 LOVE INTEREST

- SOMEONE WITH WHOM THE PROTAGONIST FALLS IN LOVE—AND WHO PROBABLY FALLS IN LOVE BACK.
- CATALYST IN THE PROTAGONIST'S INNER AND OUTER JOURNEYS.
- SUPPORTS OR RESISTS THE PROTAGONIST, DEPENDING ON THE PROTAGONIST'S COMMITMENT TO HIS GOAL.

helpingwritersbecomeauthors.com

DISCOVERING YOUR CHARACTERS

SOMETIMES YOU GET lucky when a fabulous character appears in your story, fully formed. Other times, your characters are less than cooperative and you have to work at making them likable and interesting. You're not going to find an absolute formula for writing great characters. But you can break down the great characters of literature and film to figure out what makes them tick.

Below, list your favorite characters. Consider *why* you like them and write down the traits you resonate with. Try to confine the traits to one-word tags both to simplify the exercise and to keep it as generic (and widely applicable) as possible.

(For more information on discovering your characters, see pages 51-54 of *Structuring Your Novel*.)

EXAMPLES:

- **Cora Munro:** Tough, Brave, Loyal, Open-Minded.
  (*The Last of the Mohicans* directed by Michael Mann)

- **Elizabeth Bennet:** Witty, Outgoing, Opinionated, Loyal.
  (*Pride & Prejudice* by Jane Austen)

- **Danielle de Barbarac:** Optimistic, Spunky, Passionate, Idealistic, Ethical.
  (*Ever After* directed by Andy Tennant)

- **Sue Barton:** Kind, Brave, Unprejudiced, Generous, Unflappable.
  (*Open Range* directed by Kevin Costner)

CHARACTER NAME	TRAITS THAT MAKE ME LIKE THIS CHARACTER

How is your protagonist different at the beginning of the story from how he will be

at the end? _____

_____

_____

_____

_____

_____.

What "before" scene can you include in the First Act to illustrate the personality, problems, fears, and/or weaknesses your protagonist exhibits in the beginning?

_____

_____

_____

_____

_____.

INTRODUCING THE STAKES

A S YOUR CHARACTERS walk onto the stage in the First Act, they should bring the stakes right along with them. What they *care* about—and the antagonistic forces that *threaten* what they care about—must be shown (or, at the very least, hinted at) in order to properly foreshadow the deepening conflicts.

Later in the story, you're going to have to think of the worst possible thing that could happen to your character—and then make it worse. Whatever that "worst" thing ends up being, you need to set it up in the First Act. If your character's daughter is going to be kidnapped, the First Act is the place to show readers how much she means to him. You can't up the stakes later on without something first being *at* stake.

Answer the following questions to discover and plant your story's stakes.

(For more information on introducing your story's stakes, see pages 63-66 in *Structuring Your Novel*.)

What does your protagonist care about most in the world? _____

_____.

How can you illustrate (*show*) your protagonist's devotion to what he values? __

_____.

How will the antagonistic force threaten what he values? _____

_____.

In the First Act, how can you illustrate the antagonist's threat to (or potential to

threaten) what your protagonist values? _____

_____.

Write a list of the ten worst things that could happen to your protagonist:

EXAMPLES:

- **His escape tunnel is discovered.**
  (*The Great Escape* directed by John Sturges)

- **He discovers he will die unloved and unmourned.**
  (*A Christmas Carol* by Charles Dickens)

- **She watches as the Australian POW who has aided her is crucified.**
  (*A Town Like Alice* by Nevil Shute)

1. _____.

2. _____.

3. _____.

4. _____.

5. _____.

6. _____.

7. _____.

8. _____.

9. _____.

10. _____.

Which is the most interesting for your story? _____.

How does it align with what your character cares about most?_____

_____.

INTRODUCING THE SETTINGS

SETTING SHOULD NEVER be an arbitrary choice. When you begin your story, always consider what type of settings the plot will require, then try to create the strongest reading experience with as few extraneous settings as possible. Consolidated settings will give both you and the readers less to keep track of and will allow you more opportunities for deepening the settings you do have. They'll also allow you to create thematic resonance by returning to them at key moments, thus bringing their presence in the story full circle.

Answer the following questions about your story's settings.

(For more information about setting, see pages 66-74 of *Structuring Your Novel*.)

What one setting defines your story? _____.

EXAMPLES:

- **Prison.**
  (*Rita Hayworth and the Shawshank Redemption* by Stephen King)

- **Rome.**
  (*Gladiator* directed by Ridley Scott)

- **A galaxy far, far away.**
  (*Star Wars* directed by George Lucas)

Describe the "normal world" in which your story opens: _____

_____.

EXAMPLES:

- **Sleepy, rural Meryton in Hampshire, England.**
  (*Pride & Prejudice* by Jane Austen)

- **School on Earth.**
  (*Ender's Game* by Orson Scott Card)

- **Old lady's attic.**
  (*Ratatouille* directed by Brad Bird)

How does the normal world demonstrate what your character cares about (and thus what's at stake for him)? _____

_____.

How does the normal world contrast the situation in which the character finds himself in the Second Act? _____

_____.

How can you use similar or contrasting settings to frame the beginning and end of your story? _____

_____.

EXAMPLES:

- **The Darlings' house.**
  (*Peter Pan* by J.M. Barrie)

- **The Martins' plantation.**
  (*The Patriot* directed by Roland Emmerich)

- **District 12.**
  (*The Hunger Games* by Suzanne Collins)

SETTING CHECKLIST

ALL STORIES POSSESS two kinds of setting: the concrete and the throwaway. *Concrete settings* are dictated by scenes that must take place in a specific locale.

EXAMPLES:

- The scene in which Elizabeth Bennet and Fitzwilliam Darcy are reunited, after Elizabeth's refusal of his first proposal, had to take place on the sumptuous grounds of Darcy's Pemberley estate. (*Pride & Prejudice* by Jane Austen)

- To be historically accurate, specific American Revolution battles had to take place in South Carolina. (*The Patriot* directed by Roland Emmerich)

Throwaway settings, by contrast, are *not* confined by the needs of the scene.

EXAMPLES:

- Darcy's first proposal, in a drawing room, could have taken place anywhere. (*Pride & Prejudice*)

- The militia's base could have been set anywhere. (*The Patriot*)

Whenever you write a scene with a throwaway setting, stop and think. Could you bring a new level to your scene by adding an interesting or unexpected setting? Changing the setting might be all that's needed to add depth to your scene, heighten the tension, and even lead to unanticipated story angles.

Answer the following questions about your story's settings. As you continue to fill out your structure, return to this section to add every new setting you come up with.

(For more information on concrete and throwaway settings, see pages 68-69 in *Structuring Your Novel.*)

Setting #1: _____.

Brief Description: _____

_____

_____.

Introduced in Act 1 ☐ Act 2a ☐ Act 2b ☐ Act 3 ☐

    If introduced in the first half, how can you reuse it in the second? _____

_____.

    If introduced in the second half, how can you foreshadow it in the first? _____

_____.

Concrete ☐ Throwaway ☐

    For throwaway scenes: Can you combine with an existing concrete setting? _____

_____.

    If not, list five ways to make this setting as interesting as possible:

        1. _____.

        2. _____.

        3. _____.

        4. _____.

        5. _____.

Setting #2: _____.

Brief Description: _____

_____

_____.

Introduced in Act 1 ☐ Act 2a ☐ Act 2b ☐ Act 3 ☐

    If introduced in the first half, how can you reuse it in the second? _____

    _____.

    If introduced in the second half, how can you foreshadow it in the first? _____

    _____.

Concrete ☐ Throwaway ☐

    For throwaway scenes: Can you combine with an existing concrete setting? _____

    _____.

    If not, list five ways to make this setting as interesting as possible:

        1. _____.

        2. _____.

        3. _____.

        4. _____.

        5. _____.

Setting #3: _____.

Brief Description: _____

_____

_____.

Introduced in Act 1 ☐ Act 2a ☐ Act 2b ☐ Act 3 ☐

    If introduced in the first half, how can you reuse it in the second? _____

    _____.

    If introduced in the second half, how can you foreshadow it in the first? _____

    _____.

Concrete ☐ Throwaway ☐

    For throwaway scenes: Can you combine with an existing concrete setting? _____

    _____.

    If not, list five ways to make this setting as interesting as possible:

        1. _____.

        2. _____.

        3. _____.

        4. _____.

        5. _____.

Setting #4: _____.

Brief Description: _____

_____

_____.

Introduced in Act 1 ☐ Act 2a ☐ Act 2b ☐ Act 3 ☐

    If introduced in the first half, how can you reuse it in the second? _____

    _____.

    If introduced in the second half, how can you foreshadow it in the first? _____

    _____.

Concrete ☐ Throwaway ☐

    For throwaway scenes: Can you combine with an existing concrete setting? _____

    _____.

    If not, list five ways to make this setting as interesting as possible:

        1. _____.

        2. _____.

        3. _____.

        4. _____.

        5. _____.

Setting #5: _____.

Brief Description: _____

_____

_____.

Introduced in Act 1 ☐ Act 2a ☐ Act 2b ☐ Act 3 ☐

    If introduced in the first half, how can you reuse it in the second? _____

    _____.

    If introduced in the second half, how can you foreshadow it in the first? _____

    _____.

Concrete ☐ Throwaway ☐

    For throwaway scenes: Can you combine with an existing concrete setting? _____

    _____.

    If not, list five ways to make this setting as interesting as possible:

        1. _____.

        2. _____.

        3. _____.

        4. _____.

        5. _____.

Setting #6: _____.

Brief Description: _____

_____

_____.

Introduced in Act 1 □ Act 2a □ Act 2b □ Act 3 □

If introduced in the first half, how can you reuse it in the second? _____

_____.

If introduced in the second half, how can you foreshadow it in the first? _____

_____.

Concrete □ Throwaway □

For throwaway scenes: Can you combine with an existing concrete setting? _____

_____.

If not, list five ways to make this setting as interesting as possible:

1. _____.

2. _____.

3. _____.

4. _____.

5. _____.

CHARACTERS' PERSONAL SURROUNDINGS

IF YOUR STORY allows, stage at least one scene in your character's personal surroundings—the earlier the better. Sketch the setting briefly when the character first enters it, then scatter important details throughout the scene. Is your character sloppy or neat? Rich or poor? Can readers identify his interests or hobbies from the items he has on display? Are there any clues to his backstory or his dreams for the future?

For each prominent character in your story, describe how his personal setting (house, bedroom, office, car, etc.) reveals aspects of his personality.

(For more information on your characters' personal surroundings, see pages 70-71 in *Structuring Your Novel*.)

Protagonist's personal setting: _____

_____.

What does this setting reveal about this character? _____

_____.

How can you feature this setting in your story? _____.

Antagonist's personal setting: _____

_____.

What does this setting reveal about this character? _____

_____.

How can you feature this setting in your story? _____

_____.

Love Interest's personal setting: _____

_____.

What does this setting reveal about this character? _____

_____.

How can you feature this setting in your story? _____

_____.

Sidekick's personal setting: _____

_____.

What does this setting reveal about this character? _____

_____.

How can you feature this setting in your story? _____

_____.

Mentor's personal setting: _____

_____.

What does this setting reveal about this character? _____

_____.

How can you feature this setting in your story? _____

_____.

CREATIVE EXERCISE:

List five of the most important moments in your story. Next to each moment, note the setting. Then, in a third column, write down your character's primary emotion in each scene. How does the setting reinforce that emotion?

SOMETHING TO THINK ABOUT:

1. Was your hook intriguing enough to allow you to then slow down the action and thoughtfully introduce and deepen your characters?
2. During the First Act, have you developed the salient personality points, motivations, and beliefs of your prominent characters?
3. Have you fleshed out the pertinent points of your setting, so you don't have to slow down in the Second Act to explain things?
4. Will readers have developed a bond with the characters by the end of the First Act?
5. Has your First Act made clear what the characters stand to lose in the coming conflict?
6. Is every scene in the First Act a domino that knocks into the next domino/ scene, building inexorably to the First Plot Point?

RESOURCES:

- "8 ½ Character Archetypes You Should Be Writing," K.M. Weiland, helpingwritersbecomeauthors.com/2013/12/8-½-character-archetypes-writing
- "Are You Utilizing Ugly Settings?," K.M. Weiland, helpingwritersbecome authors.com/2010/11/are-you-utilizing-ugly-settings
- "Defending Jacob: Interview with thriller author William Landay," Dorothy Thompson, helpingwritersbecomeauthors.com/SYNW-Landay

3
THE FIRST PLOT POINT

WHERE DOES IT BELONG?

25% OF THE WAY INTO YOUR STORY.

STORIES ARE A series of scenes. Some of those scenes are expected. Some of them are even purposefully repetitious for the sake of emphasis. But some scenes change everything. These game changers are the plot points. They introduce significant elements and events that alter the subsequent course of the story. Your story can have any number of plot points, some relatively minor, some shockingly huge. Plot points are what keep your story moving forward. They mix things up, keep the conflict fresh, and propel your character far away from any possibility of stagnancy.

The First Plot Point (which occurs around the 25% mark in your story) is the moment when the setup ends and everything changes for your character. This is an event that either incorporates or is directly followed by the character's *reacting* in a strong and irrevocable way. The First Plot Point marks the end of the First Act, and the character's reaction to it marks the beginning of the Second. In a sense, the First Plot Point is the Climax of the First Act.

THE INCITING AND KEY EVENTS

THE FIRST QUARTER of your story is going to hinge upon two important and irreversible moments: the Inciting Event and the Key Event—both of which directly influence (and/or sometimes *are*) the First Plot Point. The Inciting Event *sets the plot in motion*, while the Key Event *draws the protagonist into the plot*.

The Inciting Event is the moment when the story "officially" begins. But the Key Event is when the character becomes engaged *by* the Inciting Event.

EXAMPLES:

- **Inciting Event:** Brigid hires Spade's partner.
  Key Event: Spade's partner is killed and Spade is suspected.
  (*The Maltese Falcon* by Dashiell Hammett)

- **Inciting Event:** An unconscious Bourne is fished out of the ocean.
  Key Event: Someone tries to kill him.
  (*The Bourne Identity* by Robert Ludlum)

- **Inciting Event:** Marilla and Matthew decide to adopt an orphan boy.
  Key Event: They commit to keeping the orphan girl.
  (*Anne of Green Gables* by L.M. Montgomery)

The Inciting Event and the Key Event can happen anywhere in the First Act, but it's often smart to place the Inciting Event halfway through the First Act and the Key Event at the First Plot Point, since this is the moment where the character moves irrevocably away from the Normal World you've established for him in the First Act. Remember that the Inciting Event will always precede the Key Event.

Answer the following questions about your Inciting and Key Events.

(For more information about Inciting and Key Events, see pages 81-86 in *Structuring Your Novel*.)

What event sets your plot in motion? (This is your Inciting Event.) _____

_____

_____.

What event involves your protagonist in the plot? (This is Your Key Event.) _____

_____

_____.

What major event changes your story's focus at the end of the First Act? (This is

your First Plot Point.) _____.

     (Note: This answer may be the same as that for your Key Event above.)

In response to this event, what life-altering decision does your character make

that he can't turn back from? _____.

EXAMPLES:

- **Jane Eyre decides to accept a position as governess at Thornfield.**
(*Jane Eyre* by Charlotte Brontë)

- **George Bailey takes charge of the Building & Loan.**
(*It's a Wonderful Life* directed by Frank Capra)

At what point does your character leave his "normal world"? _____

_____.

What new world does he enter? _____

_____.

If he remains in the same setting, how does it change around him? _____

_____.

EXAMPLES:

- **Luke Skywalker leaves Tatooine.**
(*Star Wars: A New Hope* directed by George Lucas)

- **Boo enters the monster world, changing it to a place of chaos.**
(*Monsters, Inc.* directed by Pete Docter)

SUBPLOTS

How will the First Plot Point affect your subplot(s)?

Subplot #1: _____

_____.

Subplot #2: _____

_____.

Subplot #3: _____

_____.

FORESHADOWING

How and where in earlier chapters have you *heavily* foresha-

dowed your First Plot Point? _____

_____.

How have you *lightly* foreshadowed the First Plot Point right

before it occurred? _____

_____.

(If you don't remember what these terms mean, refer to the
Foreshadowing section on pages 32-33.)

Spotting Inciting Events and Key Events

Wuthering Heights by Emily Brontë
Inciting Event: Mr. Earnshaw brings Heathcliff home.
Key Event: Heathcliff and Cathy are separated when she has to recuperate at the Lintons.

The Great Escape directed by John Sturges
Inciting Event: The prisoners arrive in the camp.
Key Event: The prisoners start digging the first escape tunnel.

The Night Circus by Erin Morgenstern
Inciting Event: The bet is made.
Key Event: The contest begins when the circus is opened.

Star Wars directed by George Lucas
Inciting Event: Luke's uncle purchases the droids.
Key Event: Luke's aunt and uncle are murdered.

Cinder by Marissa Meyer
Inciting Event: Cinder becomes a carrier the plague.
Key Event: Cinder's stepsister contracts the plague and is quarantined.

Gladiator directed by Ridley Scott
Inciting Event: Maximus is offered the crown.
Key Event: The emperor's son tries to execute Maximus.

CREATIVE EXERCISE:

Think about some of your favorite stories. Can you spot the First Plot Points? Write a list of how the First Plot Points in these stories shake the characters' normal worlds and force them to react.

SOMETHING TO THINK ABOUT:

1. Does your First Plot Point occur around the 25% mark?
2. How is your First Plot Point an event that changes everything and becomes a personal turning point for the main character?
3. Does your First Plot Point change the story so irrevocably that even the character's surroundings (either the physical setting or the cast of supporting characters) are altered?
4. In what way does your protagonist react to your First Plot Point strongly and irretrievably?
5. Do your Inciting and Key Events take place within the first quarter of the book?
6. Does your Key Event follow the Inciting Event?
7. How does your Key Event pull the main character into the plot?

RESOURCES:

- "Plot Points and the Inciting Incident," Jim Hull, helpingwritersbecome authors.com/SYNW-Hull
- "Maximize Your Story's Inciting Event," K.M. Weiland, helpingwriters becomeauthors.com/2010/06/maximize-your-storys-inciting-event
- "How to Tell if Your Story Begins Too Soon," K.M. Weiland, helpingwritersbecomeauthors.com/2012/02/how-to-tell-if-your-story-begins-too
- "The Moment That Makes or Breaks Your Story," Larry Brooks, helping writersbecomeauthors.com/SYNW-Brooks
- "Something to Get Inciting About," Janice Hardy, helpingwritersbecome authors.com/SYNW-Hardy

4

THE FIRST HALF OF THE SECOND ACT

WHERE DOES IT BELONG?

FROM THE 25% MARK TO THE 50% MARK IN YOUR STORY.

THE SECOND ACT is the largest part of your story, comprising roughly 50%. You can simplify it by breaking it down into three segments: the First Half, the Midpoint, and the Second Half.

Every segment of a story offers its own challenges, but perhaps none leaves writers more bewildered than the Second Act. At least beginnings and endings give you a checklist of things to accomplish. The middle of the story, on the other hand, is a yawning blank. You may feel like you're entirely on your own as you try to move your characters toward where they need to be for the ending to work. Fortunately, if you pay attention to solid story structure, you'll find the middle of the story has a checklist all its own.

REACTIONS TO
THE FIRST PLOT POINT

THE FIRST HALF of the Second Act is where your characters find the time and space to react to the First Plot Point. The First Plot Point is definitive because it forces the character into irreversible reaction. That reaction, which will lead to another reaction and another and another, launches your Second Act.

To build the First Half of the Second Act, start by listing your protagonist's reactions to the First Plot Point.

(For more information on the First Half of the Second Act, see pages 89-94 in *Structuring Your Novel*.)

What is your protagonist's reaction to the new or altered setting in the Second Act?__

_____.

What is his reaction to the thwarting of his story goal in the First Plot Point? _____

_____.

What is his new or altered goal in the aftermath of the First Plot Point? _____

_____.

How is your protagonist now *reacting* to pressure from the antagonist? _____

_____.

How is the protagonist currently at a disadvantage in the conflict with the antagonist?

_____.

In what ways does the antagonist currently control the conflict? _____

_____.

REACTIONS THROUGHOUT THE FIRST HALF

FOR THE NEXT quarter of the book, until the Midpoint, your protagonist will be taking action, but all his actions are a *response* (in one form or another) to what's happened to him. He's trying to regain his balance, trying to figure out where his life is supposed to go next.

The First Half of the Second Act will begin immediately after the First Plot Point. Your character will react to the events of the plot point in such a way that he can never go back to the way things were. The antagonistic force responds, and again the character is forced to react. The cycle repeats itself as many times and with as many variations as necessary until the story reaches the Midpoint.

Answer the following questions about your protagonist's actions throughout the First Half of the Second Act.

How does the protagonist begin to prepare (knowingly or unknowingly) to better

equip himself for the conflict? _____

_____ .

With what previously introduced and/or foreshadowed characters does the

protagonist deepen his relationships? _____

_____ .

What complications arise from the protagonist's incomplete understanding of the

conflict? _____ .

What new information will the protagonist learn? _____

_____ .

What secrets will he uncover? _____

_____ .

How is he on the right track? _____

_____ .

How is he on the wrong track? _____

_____ .

SUBPLOTS

How will your subplot(s) progress in the First Half of the Second Act?

Subplot #1: _____

_____.

In what way is your protagonist (or the subplot's "lead" character) in reaction mode at this stage in the subplot?

_____

_____.

Subplot #2: _____

_____.

In what way is your protagonist (or the subplot's "lead" character) in reaction mode at this stage in the subplot?

_____

_____.

Subplot #3: _____

_____.

In what way is your protagonist (or the subplot's "lead" character) in reaction mode at this stage in the subplot?

_____

_____.

THE FIRST PINCH POINT
WHERE DOES IT BELONG?

AT THE 37% MARK.

Halfway through the First Half of the Second Act (around the 3/8th mark), your character will run afoul of the First Pinch Point. This is a scene in which the antagonist is given a chance to flex his muscles and impress readers (and probably the protagonist as well) with his scary might. This moment serves primarily as a set up to the protagonist's change of tactics in the Midpoint by reminding readers of the antagonist's power. But it also raises the stakes and foreshadows the Climax. Its focus will always be that of the central conflict, rather than a subplot.

Answer the following questions about your story's First Pinch Point.

(For more on the First Pinch Point, see pages 91-92 in *Structuring Your Novel*.)

What happens at the 3/8th mark to emphasize the antagonist's power and control?

_____

_____.

EXAMPLES:

- Elizabeth re-encounters Darcy at his aunt's estate.
  (*Pride & Prejudice* by Jane Austen)

- Highprince Dalinar is investigated by his nemesis as part of a would-be assassination of the king.
  (*The Way of Kings* by Brandon Sanderson)

- The Emperor tells Darth Vader to focus on Luke Skywalker as their new enemy.
  (*The Empire Strikes Back* directed by Irvin Kershner)

How does this event affect the central conflict? _____

_____.

Is the protagonist present for this scene (or is it told from the antagonist's point of view)?

_____

_____.

Is the antagonist present for this scene (or is his presence only *felt* by the protagonist)?

_____

_____.

How does this event help the protagonist better understand the true nature of the conflict? _____

_____.

How does this event begin to evolve the protagonist out of his reactive mindset?

_____

_____.

CREATIVE EXERCISE:

Write a list of five different ways in which your protagonist could respond to the First Plot Point. How would these different reactions alter the course of the First Half of the Second Act—and your entire story?

SOMETHING TO THINK ABOUT:

1. Do your characters react promptly and strongly to the events of the First Plot Point?
2. In the Second Half of the Second Act, how does your protagonist deal with **a)** the main antagonistic force and **b)** the world in general?
3. How are your protagonist's reactions varied throughout this second quarter of the story?
4. How do your protagonist's reactions in this section move the plot forward and deepen the weave of scenes, subplots, and themes?
5. What skills or items necessary for the final battle in the Third Act does your protagonist gain in this section?
6. At the First Pinch Point, how is your protagonist pressured by the antagonist?

RESOURCES:

- "Action and Reaction: The Building Blocks of Story Structure," K.M. Weiland, helpingwritersbecomeauthors.com/2013/08/action-reaction-building-blocks-story-structure
- "Visceral Reactions: Emotional Pay Dirt or Fast Track to Melodrama?" Angela Ackerman, helpingwritersbecomeauthors.com/2012/05/visceral-reactions-emotional-pay-dirt
- "Action and Reaction: The Pistons Powering Your Story," K.M. Weiland, helpingwritersbecomeauthors.com/2011/11/posts-9
- "How Story Structure Prevents 'Saggy Middle' Syndrome," K.M. Weiland, helpingwritersbecomeauthors.com/2013/08/story-structure-prevents-saggy-middle-syndrome

5
THE MIDPOINT

WHERE DOES IT BELONG?

50% OF THE WAY INTO YOUR STORY.

HALFWAY THROUGH THE Second Act, something marvelous happens. There you are, minding your own business, toiling along in the seemingly endless desert of the Second Act, when—*whap! bang! shazam!*—everything changes all over again. Legendary director Sam Peckinpah talked about how he always looked for a "centerpiece" on which to "hang" his story. That centerpiece is your second major plot point, the Midpoint, which divides your Second Act.

The Midpoint is what keeps your Second Act from dragging. It's what caps the *reactions* in the first half of the book and sets up the chain of *actions* that will lead the characters into the Third Act. In many ways, the Midpoint is a second Inciting Event. Like the first Inciting Event, it directly influences the plot. It changes the paradigm of the story, and it requires a definitive and story-altering response from the characters. The largest difference is that the character's response is no longer just a reaction. This is where he begins to take charge of the story and act out against the antagonistic force.

Your Story's Centerpiece

YOU CAN ENVISION the Midpoint as a turn in your story's row of dominoes. When the line of reactions from the First Half of the Second Act finally whacks into that domino at the turn, it begins a whole new line of falling dominoes. This is a big moment in the story, a major scene. It has to be the logical outcome of the previous scenes, but it should also be dramatically new and different from anything that has come before.

Answer the following questions about your story's Midpoint.

(For more information about the Midpoint, see pages 94-99 in *Structuring Your Novel*.)

What major event occurs in the middle of your story? _____

_____.

Examples:

- **The capture of the main characters.**
  (*Furies of Calderon* by Jim Butcher)

- **A battle.**
  (*The Magnificent Seven* directed by John Sturges)

- **The death of an important character.**
  (*Dragon Seed* by Pearl S. Buck)

In thinking of this event as your story's "centerpiece," how can you make it appro-

priately exciting, colorful, and dramatic? _____

_____.

How does this event change your protagonist's perception of the antagonist? _____

_____.

How does this event change your protagonist's perception of the conflict? _____

_____ .

How does this event change your protagonist's perception of himself? _____

_____ .

How does this event and your protagonist's personal revelations shift him out of a

reactive phase into an active one by allowing him to take more control of the conflict?

_____

_____ .

SUBPLOTS

How will the Midpoint bring your protagonist (or the "lead" character in your subplot) to a new understanding about your subplot(s)?

Subplot #1: _____

_____.

    Will this new understanding be a direct or indirect result

    of the revelations in the Midpoint? _____.

    How? _____

_____.

Subplot #2: _____

_____.

    Will this new understanding be a direct or indirect result

    of the revelations in the Midpoint? _____.

    How? _____

_____.

Subplot #3: _____

_____.

    Will this new understanding be a direct or indirect result

    of the revelations in the Midpoint? _____.

    How? _____

_____.

FORESHADOWING:

How and where in earlier chapters have you *heavily* foreshadowed

your Midpoint? _____

_____.

How have you *lightly* foreshadowed the Midpoint right before it

occurred? _____

_____.

CREATIVE EXERCISE:

Think about some of your favorite stories. Can you spot the Midpoint? Write a list of how the Midpoint in these stories brings the characters to a revelation about themselves and the conflict.

SOMETHING TO THINK ABOUT:

1. Does your Midpoint land near the halfway point in your story?
2. In what way is your Midpoint new and fresh in comparison to the previous scenes?
3. Is what happens at your Midpoint a natural outflow of the previous scenes?
4. Is the Midpoint a personal catalyst for the main character?
5. How does the Midpoint force your character to change his *modus operandi* and take more control of the conflict?

RESOURCES:

- "The Mirror Moment: A Method for Both Plotters and Pantsers," James Scott Bell, helpingwritersbecomeauthors.com/2014/03/plotters-and-pantsers
- "A Matter of Timing: Positioning Your Major Plot Points Within Your Story," K.M. Weiland, helpingwritersbecomeauthors.com/2013/10/matter-timing-positioning-major-plot-points-within-story
- "What Are Plot Points?" K.M. Weiland, helpingwritersbecomeauthors.com/2013/08/plot-points
- "10 Ways Plot Structure Influences Character Arc," K.M. Weiland, helpingwritersbecomeauthors.com/2013/08/10-ways-plot-structure-influences-character-arc
- "Beating the Sloggy, Saggy, Soggy Middle," Heather Webb, helpingwritersbecomeauthors.com/SYNW-Webb

6

THE SECOND HALF OF THE SECOND ACT

WHERE DOES IT BELONG?

FROM THE 50% MARK TO THE 75% MARK IN YOUR STORY.

THE SECOND HALF of the Second Act is where your plot really begins popping. Your main character caps the dramatic event at the Midpoint with his decision to stop reacting and start acting. Almost always, this is born of a personal revelation, even if the character can't yet quite put it into concrete terms. As of the Midpoint, he's becoming someone new. He's realizing his full power and stretching his wings to discover what he can do with that power. His crippling inner problems are still getting in the way, but, at the very least, he's realizing he has to do something either about or in spite of them.

Because the Second Half of the Second Act will lead right into the slugfest of the Third Act, this is your last chance to get all your playing pieces into position. You have to set up the line of dominoes that will knock into the Third Plot Point at the 75% mark, and you do that by creating a series of actions from the main character. Although he's not likely to be in control of the situation, he's at least moving forward and calling a few shots of his own, instead of taking it and taking it from the antagonistic force.

ACTIONS AFTER THE MIDPOINT

THE SECOND HALF of the Second Act begins with a strong action from the protagonist. He rises from the drama and trauma of the Midpoint and grits his teeth. He responds with an action that fights back.

The series of actions in the Second Half of the Second Act mirrors the series of reactions in the First Half. In a sense, of course, the character is still reacting (if you peer too closely at the line between action and reaction, it can blur very quickly). But the emphasis is on his own inner purpose now, rather than his need to raise his shields and duck his head. He's not yet in control of his destiny, but at least now he's trying to do something about his lack of control.

Answer the following questions about your protagonist's reaction to the Midpoint. (For more, see pages 103-112 in *Structuring Your Novel*.)

How is your protagonist's resolve to conquer the conflict strengthened after the

Midpoint? _____

_____.

EXAMPLES:

- **Intensifying the attacks on the nobles.**
  (*Mistborn* by Brandon Sanderson)

- **Searching for the truth about the dagger.**
  (*Prince of Persia* directed by Mike Newell)

- **Reuniting the militia.**
  (*The Patriot* directed by Roland Emmerich)

What decision does the protagonist make as a result? _____

_____.

What strong action does he take to enter the second half of the book? _____

_____.

How has the protagonist's emphasis shifted from defense to offense? _____

_____.

List all the actions you think your protagonist might take after the Midpoint and throughout the rest of the Second Act: _____

_____

_____

_____

_____

_____

_____

_____

_____

_____

_____

_____

_____

_____.

How will the antagonist react to the protagonist's renewed attack? _____

_____.

What partial or apparent victory will your protagonist achieve by the end of the

Second Act? _____

_____.

As a result of this seeming victory, how will the character's story goal appear to

be within his reach? _____

_____.

YOUR PROTAGONIST'S EVOLUTION

SOME STORIES PURPOSEFULLY leave their characters unchanged in a changing world to underline a point. But in most stories, the fires through which we force our characters should cause them to learn hard truths and grow from reaction to action in perhaps painful, but definitely necessary ways.

Your character's arc of personal growth is what drives your story. As you enter the second half of the book, be on guard against your character's reacting to similar situations in the same way over and over again. If he is, then you've allowed him to slide into stagnation.

Check yourself by answering the following questions.

How will your protagonist put into action the lessons he has learned in the story's

first half? _____

_____ .

What new information will he learn in the second half? _____

_____

_____ .

What secrets will he uncover? _____

_____ .

How is he on the right track at this point in the story? _____

_____ .

How does this differ from your answer in the first half (page 68)? _____

_____ .

How is he on the wrong track at this point in the story? _____

_____ .

How does this differ from your answer in the first half (page 68)? _____

_____.

SUBPLOTS

How will your subplot(s) progress in the Second Half of the Second Act?

Subplot #1: _____

_____.

    In what way is your protagonist (or the subplot's "lead" character) shifting into an active role in this subplot?

_____

_____.

Subplot #2: _____

_____.

    In what way is your protagonist (or the subplot's "lead" character) shifting into an active role in this subplot?

_____

_____.

Subplot #3: _____

_____.

    In what way is your protagonist (or the subplot's "lead" character) shifting into an active role in this subplot?

_____

_____.

BEFORE AND AFTER
HOW STORIES CHANGE CHARACTERS

 EMMA:

BEFORE: Determinedly single, convinced of her matchmaking skills, interferes in friends' lives.

AFTER: In love, humbled by matchmaking failures, remorseful for harming friends.

CASABLANCA:

BEFORE: Bitter after failed love affair, determined not to get involved in other people's problems, alcoholic.

AFTER: Learns to forgive, willing to surrender lost love, fights for a greater cause.

GREAT EXPECTATIONS:

BEFORE: Uneducated, believes life owes him something, hurts those who love him.

AFTER: Experienced in the ways of the world, humbled by his disappointments, seeks forgiveness from those he's hurt.

IT'S A WONDERFUL LIFE:

BEFORE: Wants to do something big with his life, restless with small town life, trapped by responsibilities.

AFTER: Realizes his accomplishments have been important, accepts his family and friends as the most important thing in his life, embraces ability to help others.

THE GREAT GATSBY:

BEFORE: Country boy, inexperienced in the ways of the world, idealistic about people.

AFTER: Experienced in the ways of the wealthy, world weary, cynical about people.

helpingwritersbecomeauthors.com

THE SECOND PINCH POINT
WHERE DOES IT BELONG?

At the 62% mark.

HALFWAY THROUGH THE Second Half of the Second Act (roundabout the 5/8th mark) we find the Second Pinch Point. Like the First Pinch Point, this scene showcases the antagonist, either personally or in some manifestation that emphasizes his power and his potential ability to defeat the protagonist. This point serves most of the same purposes as the First Pinch Point, including ramping up the stakes and foreshadowing the final battle between the protagonist and the antagonist.

To identify your Second Pinch Point, answer the following questions.

(For more information on the Second Pinch Point, see page 106 in *Structuring Your Novel*.)

What happens to emphasize the antagonist's power and control? _____

_____.

EXAMPLES:

- Jane's "dream" of the ghost who enters her bedroom and rends her bridal veil.
  (*Jane Eyre* by Charlotte Brontë)

- Darth Vader's hiring the bounty hunters.
  (*The Empire Strikes Back* directed by Irvin Kershner)

- The revelation that the moon queen is preparing to invade Earth.
  (*Cinder* by Marissa Meyer)

How does this event affect the central conflict? _____

_____.

Is the protagonist present for this scene (or is it told from the antagonist's POV)?

_____.

Is the antagonist present for this scene (or is his presence only felt by the protagonist)?

_____.

How does this event emphasize the antagonist's power and his ability to defeat the

protagonist?_____

_____.

How does this event foreshadow the final battle? _____

_____.

How does this event spur the protagonist even further out of his reactive mindset?

_____

_____.

How does this event raise the stakes for the protagonist? _____

_____.

CREATIVE EXERCISE:

It's not enough to tell readers your character is becoming more empowered. Think of three actions your character can take that will contrast his misconception-based reactions in the first half of the book.

SOMETHING TO THINK ABOUT:

1. What series of actions will the main character take in the Second Half of the Second Act?
2. How does overcoming his ignorance about the conflict, the antagonist, and himself allow him to take a more active role in controlling the conflict?
3. How does your Second Pinch Point reaffirm the antagonist's presence and power within the story?
4. What revelations will your character discover in the Second Half of the Second Act?
5. Which of your protagonist's problems will be resolved in this section?
6. Which major problems—both inner and outer—will remain to be solved during the Third Act?
7. How might the problems that *are* solved in the Second Half of the Second Act serve to exacerbate or bring clearer focus to the true underlying conflicts?

RESOURCES:

- "3 Ways to Add Repetition That Pleases Readers," Elizabeth Spann Craig, helpingwritersbecomeauthors.com/2013/05/3-ways-to-add-repetition-that-pleases
- "Two Surefire Symptoms of a Static Character," K.M. Weiland, helping writersbecomeauthors.com/2012/01/two-surefire-symptoms-of-static
- "It's What Your Characters *Do* That Defines Them," K.M. Weiland, helpingwritersbecomeauthors.com/2009/08/its-what-your-characters-do-that
- "How the Antagonist Affects Character Arc," K.M. Weiland, helping writersbecomeauthors.com/2013/12/antagonist-affects-character-arc
- "Second Act Problems," Steven Pressfield, helpingwritersbecome authors.com/SYNW-Pressfield

7
THE THIRD ACT

WHERE DOES IT BELONG?

FROM THE 75% MARK TO THE 100% MARK IN YOUR STORY.

THE THIRD ACT occupies the final quarter of the book, beginning around or slightly before the 75% mark and continuing until the end. This is a relatively small portion of the story, particularly when you think about all that must be accomplished within it. One of the reasons the Third Act will pick up the pace compared to the previous acts is the simple necessity of cramming in everything that needs to be addressed before the book runs out of time and space.

All the characters must be assembled. Subplots must be satisfactorily tied off. Foreshadowing must be fulfilled. Both the hero and the antagonist (if there is one) must have time to put into play the final aspects of their plans. The hero must face his inner demons and complete his character arc in concert with the final conflict with the antagonistic force. And then everything must be capped with a satisfying denouement.

That's a lot to accomplish in a mere 25% of the book, so there's no time to waste. In the Third Act, you can see one of the primary benefits of structure: for the story to work, all the pieces in the First and Second Acts must be in place to lay the foundation for the finale.

THE THIRD PLOT POINT

The Third Act will begin with another life-changing plot point. This plot point, more than any of those that preceded it, will set the protagonist's feet on the path toward the final conflict in the Climax. From here on in, your clattering dominoes will form a straight line as your protagonist hurtles toward his inevitable clash with the antagonistic force. The Third Act as a whole is full of big and important scenes, so by comparison its opening plot point is often less defined than the plot points that marked the First and Second Acts. However, its thrust must be just as adamant.

This will lead right into your character's low point. The thing he wants most in the world will be almost within his grasp—only to be dashed away, smashing him down even lower than before. The Climax will be the period in which he rises from the ashes, ready to do battle from a place of inner wholeness. The Third Plot Point is the place from which he must rise.

Identify and strengthen your Third Plot Point by answering the following questions.

(For more information on the Third Plot Point, see pages 116-122 in *Structuring Your Novel*.)

What event shatters the protagonist's seeming moment of victory? _____

_____ .

EXAMPLES:

- Ra's Al Ghul announces his intentions to destroy Gotham, then burns Bruce Wayne's mansion and leaves him for dead.
(*Batman Begins* directed by Christopher Nolan)

- Mattie discovers the murderer Tom Chaney and is subsequently captured by Ned Pepper's gang of outlaws.
(*True Grit* by Charles Portis)

- Lucy learns that her impulsive romantic interlude in Italy has been immortalized in Miss Lavish's novel.
(*A Room With a View* by E.M. Forster)

How does the Third Plot Point crush your character in a moment of defeat? _____

_____.

How does the protagonist's personal weakness cause this moment? _____

_____.

What does your protagonist question about his overall goal? _____

_____.

What does your protagonist question about himself, his abilities, and his motivations

up to this point?_____

_____.

What personal revelations does he have? _____

_____.

What personal decisions does he make in reaction to those revelations? _____

_____.

What prompts him to rise again and reengage in the conflict? _____

_____.

How is the protagonist different after this "death/rebirth" phase? _____

_____.

SUBPLOTS

How will the Third Plot Point bring your protagonist (or the "lead" character in your subplot) to a new understanding about your subplot(s)?

Subplot #1: _____

_____.

  Will this new understanding be a direct or indirect result

  of the revelations in the Third Plot Point? _____

  _____.

Subplot #2: _____

_____.

  Will this new understanding be a direct or indirect result

  of the revelations in the Third Plot Point? _____

  _____.

Subplot #3: _____

_____.

  Will this new understanding be a direct or indirect result

  of the revelations in the Third Plot Point? _____

  _____.

FORESHADOWING

How and where in earlier chapters have you *heavily* fore-

shadowed your Third Plot Point? _____

_____ .

How have you *lightly* foreshadowed the Third Plot Point right

before it occurred? _____

_____ .

AFTER THE THIRD PLOT POINT

CHARACTER AND CHANGE. That's what story is all about. We take a person and we force him onto a journey that will change him forever, usually for the better. In the First Act, he starts out in a less-than-fulfilled, probably personally stunted place. He has certain beliefs that are holding him back from what he *needs*, from the thing that will cause him to change into this better, more enlightened, more empowered person.

Personal transformations are always at the heart of strong character arcs. Without one, your character will remain static, the plot will fall flat, and readers will be left to wonder, *Why did any of that matter?*

To solidify your character's arc, ask yourself the following questions.

(For more information on character arcs in the Third Act, see pages 117-119 in *Structuring Your Novel.*)

How is your protagonist different now from how he was in the beginning of the

story? _____

_____.

EXAMPLES:

- **Instead of trying to eliminate or manipulate Buzz, Woody welcomes him as a partner and friend.**
  (*Toy Story* directed by John Lasseter)

- **Instead of putting wealth ahead of everything else, Scrooge buys food and gifts for others.**
  (*A Christmas Carol* by Charles Dickens)

- **Instead of bowing to the will of others in order to be loved, Jane claims her independence.**
  (*Jane Eyre* by Charlotte Brontë)

What scene can you include in the Third Act to illustrate how your protagonist's personality, problems, fears, and/or weaknesses have evolved? _____

_____

_____

_____.

What new and strengthened action does the protagonist take against the antagonistic force after the Third Plot Point? _____

_____.

How does he assemble all the skills, tools, and allies he gained throughout the story, in preparation for the Climax? _____

_____

_____.

Which of these playing pieces will need to be present in the final showdown? _____

_____.

How will you get them there? _____

_____.

SUBPLOTS

Which of your subplots can you tie off before the Climax—and how?

Subplot #1: _____

_____.

Subplot #2: _____

_____.

Subplot #3: _____

_____.

CHARACTER DEATH CHECKLIST

BECAUSE THE THIRD Plot Point is a symbolic representation of your protagonist's spiritual death and rebirth, this plot point often features either literal or figurative death.

If one of your characters dies here (or at any other moment in your story), ask yourself the following questions.

(For more information on how to successfully kill off characters, see pages 153-157 in *Structuring Your Novel*.)

Why is the death necessary? _____

_____.

How does the death affect the other characters? _____

_____.

How does the death advance the plot? _____

_____.

What would happen to the story and the other characters if this character didn't die?

_____.

Will the death shock readers? _____

_____.

Will the shock prevent the purpose of the death from resonating with readers?

_____.

Can you mitigate the shock by foreshadowing the death? _____

_____.

Can you foreshadow the death explicitly with a reference to the possibility of

the character's dying? _____

_____.

Can you foreshadow the death implicitly through tone or a general sense of

foreboding?_____

_____.

Do you want your story to have a sad ending?
☐ Yes ☐ No

If no, ask yourself:
If the death occurs early in the story (Third Plot Point or earlier), how will

the remaining characters' actions in the Climax make the death matter? _____

_____.

If the death occurs late in the story (Climax or after), what affirming or

empowering note can you find to shine a light through the grief? _____

_____.

How to Kill a Character

The Checklist

Good Reasons to Kill a Character

✓ **It advances the plot.**
(Melanie in Gone With the Wind)

✓ **It fulfills the doomed character's personal goal.**
(Obi-Wan in A New Hope)

✓ **It motivates other characters.**
(Uncle Ben in Spider-Man)

✓ **It's a fitting recompense for the character's actions up to this point.**
(Heathcliff in Wuthering Heights)

✓ **It emphasizes the theme.**
(Everybody in Flowers of War)

✓ **It creates realism within the story world.**
(Everybody in The Great Escape)

✓ **It removes an extraneous character.**
(Danny in Pearl Harbor)

Bad Reasons to Kill a Character

✗ **Shocking readers just for the sake of shocking them.**
(Shock value isn't without its, well, value, but not every author is Alfred Hitchcock and not every story is Psycho.)

✗ **Making readers sad just for the sake of making them sad.**
(An old saw says, "If they cry, they buy." But readers never appreciate being tortured without good reason.)

✗ **Removing an extraneous character.**
(Yes, this is also a good reason. But double-check. If the character is extraneous, first verify he really belongs in this story in the first place.)

CREATIVE EXERCISE:

Think about some of your favorite stories. Can you spot the Third Plot Point? Write a list of how the Third Plot Point in these stories brings the characters to a revelation about themselves and the conflict.

SOMETHING TO THINK ABOUT:

1. Does your Third Act begin around the 75% mark?
2. How is your Third Plot Point an upheaval of the gains your protagonist thought he had made up to now?
3. From its opening plot point onward, does your Third Act pick up speed and refuse to slow down?
4. Is your Third Act thoughtful enough in its first moments to allow all the extra pieces to be either tied off and set out of the way or assembled for the showdown?

RESOURCES:

- "5 Elements of Story Structure," J.E. Fishman, helpingwritersbecome authors.com/2013/01/5-elements-of-story-structure
- "The All-Important Link Between Theme and Character Progression," K.M. Weiland, helpingwritersbecomeauthors.com/2008/06/all-important-link-between-theme-and
- "What's the Most Important Moment in Your Character's Arc?," K.M. Weiland, helpingwritersbecomeauthors.com/2012/12/whats-most-important-moment-in-your
- "How to Successfully Kill a Character: The Checklist," K.M. Weiland, helpingwritersbecomeauthors.com/2014/01/kill-a-character
- "Creating Characters That Make Readers Cry," Jody Hedlund, helpingwritersbecomeauthors.com/SYNW-Hedlund

8

THE CLIMAX

WHERE DOES IT BELONG?

FROM THE 90% MARK TO THE 98% MARK IN YOUR STORY.

IN SOME STORIES, the Climax will involve a drawn-out physical battle. In others, the Climax might be nothing more than a simple admission that changes everything for the protagonist. Almost always, it is a moment of revelation for the main character. Depending on the needs of the story, the protagonist will come to a life-changing epiphany directly before, during, or after the Climax. He will then act definitively upon that revelation, capping the change in his character arc and ending the primary conflict, either physically or spiritually, or both.

The Climax occurs at the end of the Third Act and comprises approximately the last 10% of the book. More often than not, the Climactic Moment at the end of the Climax will be the penultimate scene, just before the denouement. Since the Climax says everything there is to be said, with the exception of a little emotional mopping up, there's no need for the story to continue long after its completion.

YOUR STORY'S CLIMAX

THE FOUNDATION OF your slam-bang finale has to be built into the story—the plot and the characters—that preceded it. The Climax is where you have to pull out your big guns. This needs to be a series of scenes that wows readers. Dig deep for your most extraordinary and imaginative ideas. Instead of just a fistfight, why not a fistfight on top of a moving train? Instead of just a declaration of love, why not a declaration in the middle of a presidential inauguration?

Answer the following questions to refine your story's Climax.

(For more information about the Climax, see pages 125-133 in *Structuring Your Novel*.)

What form will the final confrontation between the protagonist and the antagonistic

force take? _____

_____.

EXAMPLES:

- **Naval battle.**
  (*Master and Commander* by Patrick O'Brian)

- **Horserace.**
  (*The Rievers* by William Faulkner)

- **Filibuster.**
  (*Mr. Smith Goes to Washington* directed by Frank Capra)

Where will your Climax take place? _____.

How does this setting symbolically emphasize the central conflict and the theme?

_____.

How does this setting physically or emotionally make the confrontation with the

antagonist more difficult? _____

_____.

How will the protagonist's new resolve and understanding of truths about himself and the world be challenged one more time? _____

_____ .

How will the protagonist respond to this challenge? _____

_____ .

Will the protagonist defeat the antagonistic force—or be defeated? _____ .

How is the victory, by either side, achieved? _____

_____ .

What one moment have readers been waiting for since the beginning of the story?

_____

_____ .

EXAMPLES:

- **The kiss between the romantic leads.**
  (*North & South* by Elizabeth Gaskell)

- **The White Witch's death.**
  (*The Lion, the Witch, and the Wardrobe* by C.S. Lewis)

- **The return of the hero's memory.**
  (*Random Harvest* by James Hilton)

How can you deliver this moment? _____

_____ .

FORESHADOWING

How and where in earlier chapters have you *heavily* foreshadowed our Climax and Climactic Moment? _____

_____

_____.

How have you *lightly* foreshadowed the Climax and Climactic Moment right before they occurred? _____

_____

_____.

Now that you know how your climactic battle will play out, how and where can you foreshadow the form of the final confrontation earlier in the story? _____

_____

_____.

How and where can you foreshadow the Climax's setting? _____

_____

_____.

List five things readers will expect from your Climax by the time they've read this far:

1. _____.

2. _____.

3. _____.

4. _____.

5. _____.

Which do you *have* to fulfill for the story to make sense and satisfy readers?
☐ 1 ☐ 2 ☐ 3 ☐ 4 ☐ 5

How can you introduce complications in your Climax that readers *won't* expect? _____

_____.

Will your story include a faux Climax? If so, what will it be? _____

_____.

EXAMPLES:

- **Woody and Buzz must first defeat Sid, *then* the threat of being left behind by the moving van.**
  (*Toy Story* directed by John Lasseter)

- **George Bailey must defeat first his own wish to be unborn, *then* the remaining discrepancies in his business accounts.**
  (*It's a Wonderful Life* directed by Frank Capra)

What lessons will the protagonist learn in the faux Climax that will prepare him

for the true Climax? _____

_____.

Does your character have more than one antagonistic force to defeat? _____

_____.

CREATIVE EXERCISE:

Brainstorm five possible endings for your story. Maybe in one version the bad guy wins. Or the hero wins but doesn't get the girl. What do each of these alternate endings offer that your original ending doesn't?

SOMETHING TO THINK ABOUT:

1. Does your Climax begin around the 90% mark and end only a scene or two away from the last page?
2. Is your Climax more than just one scene—is it a sequence of scenes that builds up to the important Climactic Moment?
3. How does your Climax decisively end the primary conflict with the antagonistic force?
4. How is your Climax the direct result of the protagonist's personal revelation about his character arc?
5. Does your story have so many layers of conflict that it requires a "faux" Climax leading up to the Climax proper?

RESOURCES:

- "Have You Invited Enough Characters to Your Climax?" K.M. Weiland, helpingwritersbecomeauthors.com/2013/12/invited-enough-characters-storys-Climax
- "How to Structure a Whammy of a Climax," K.M. Weiland, helping writersbecomeauthors.com/2013/08/structure-whammy-Climax
- "Are Your Bad Guys Dying in the Right Order?" K.M. Weiland, helpingwritersbecomeauthors.com/2013/05/are-your-bad-guys-dying-in-right-order
- "The Inevitable Ending You Know Is Coming," C.S. Lakin, helpingwriters becomeauthors.com/SYNW-Lakin
- "Special Scenes: Climax," Darcy Pattinson, helpingwritersbecome authors.com/SYNW-Pattinson

9

THE RESOLUTION

WHERE DOES IT BELONG?

FROM THE 98% MARK TO THE 100% MARK IN YOUR STORY.

THE RESOLUTION WILL begin directly after the Climax and continue until the last page. After all the emotional stress of the Climax, readers want a moment to relax. They want to see the character rising, dusting off his pants, and moving on with life. They want to catch a glimpse of how the ordeals of the previous three acts have *changed* your character; they want a preview of the new life he will live in the aftermath of the conflict. And, if you've done your job right, they'll want this extra scene for no other reason than to spend *just a little more time* with these characters they've grown to love. As its name suggests, the Resolution is where everything is *resolved*.

Resolutions can vary in length, but shorter is generally better. Your story is already essentially over. You don't want to try readers' patience by wasting their time, and you definitely don't want to stunt their sense of the story by tying off every loose end too perfectly. The length of your Resolution will depend on a couple of factors, the most important being the number of remaining loose ends. Optimally, you will have used the scenes leading up to your Climax to resolve as many subplots as possible, which will free up your Resolution to take care of only the essentials.

PLANNING YOUR RESOLUTION

CREATING THE PERFECT ending isn't easy, but you can boil it down to one essential objective: leave readers with a feeling of satisfaction. How do you do that? If you can give readers a sense of continuing motion in your characters' lives—a sense of progression even after all the big plot issues have been resolved—you will be able both to create a feeling of realism and to engage your readers' imaginations in filling in the "rest of the story."

The Resolution is not just the ending of *this* story, but also the beginning of the story the characters will live in after readers have closed the back cover. It performs its two greatest duties in capping the current story, while still promising that the characters' lives will continue.

Craft your Resolution by answering the following questions.

(For more information on the Resolution, see pages 137-164 in *Structuring Your Novel*.)

How much time passes between your Climactic Moment and the Resolution?

How many:

_____ Hours

_____ Days

_____ Months

_____ Years

What is your protagonist's reaction to the events of the Climax? _____

_____

_____

_____

_____.

What feeling do you want to leave readers with when they close the book?

- ☐ Optimism
- ☐ Pessimism
- ☐ Defeat
- ☐ Fear
- ☐ Hope
- ☐ Sadness
- ☐ Joy
- ☐ Cynicism
- ☐ Idealism
- ☐ Anger
- ☐ Awe
- ☐ Disappointment
- ☐ Remorse
- ☐ Contempt
- ☐ Aggression
- ☐ Other _____.

How can you achieve this tone in your final scene? _____

_____.

What final characteristic moment, featuring your protagonist, will help establish

this tone? _____

_____.

What loose ends remain to be tied off?

- ☐ Romantic Subplot.

    How will you tie it off? _____.

- ☐ Career Subplot:

    How will you tie it off? _____.

☐ Family Subplot:

　　How will you tie it off? _____.

☐ Best Friend Subplot:

　　How will you tie it off? _____.

☐ Minor Character Arc Subplot:

　　How will you tie it off? _____.

☐ Other: _____

　　How will you tie it off? _____.

How can you bring each of your important characters onstage (or at least refer to them) one more time?

　　Antagonist: _____.

　　Love Interest: _____.

　　Sidekick: _____.

　　Mentor: _____.

　　Other Important Characters: _____

_____

_____.

What is your protagonist's new goal for his life *after* the story? _____

_____.

How can your Resolution make use of settings that reflect or contrast those in your

opening chapters? _____

_____

_____.

EXAMPLES:

- **The Darlings' house.**
  (*Peter Pan* by J.M. Barrie)

- **The Martins' plantation.**
  (*The Patriot* directed by Roland Emmerich)

- **District 12.**
  (*The Hunger Games* by Suzanne Collins)

CLOSING LINE CHECKLIST

LIKE FIRST LINES, last lines aren't all that memorable in themselves. Their memorability isn't nearly as important as is the *feeling* with which they leave readers. What is it about great closing lines that makes stories resonate with us? How do closing lines help embed stories in our minds so we will carry them with us long after we've closed the back covers?

Your closing line will depend greatly on the story that precedes it: its tone, pacing, and the mood you want to strike with its ending. Use the following questions to get the most out of your closing line.

(For more information on closing lines, see pages 141-144 in *Structuring Your Novel*.)

How does your closing line offer a sense of finality to the story? _____

_____.

How does your closing line *also* offer a sense that your characters' lives will continue

after the story?_____

_____.

How does your closing line reinforce the theme? _____

_____.

Do the lines leading up to your closing line slow the pace with longer sentences?_____

_____.

Is your closing line itself a punchy sentence that acts as a final period at the end of

your story? _____

_____.

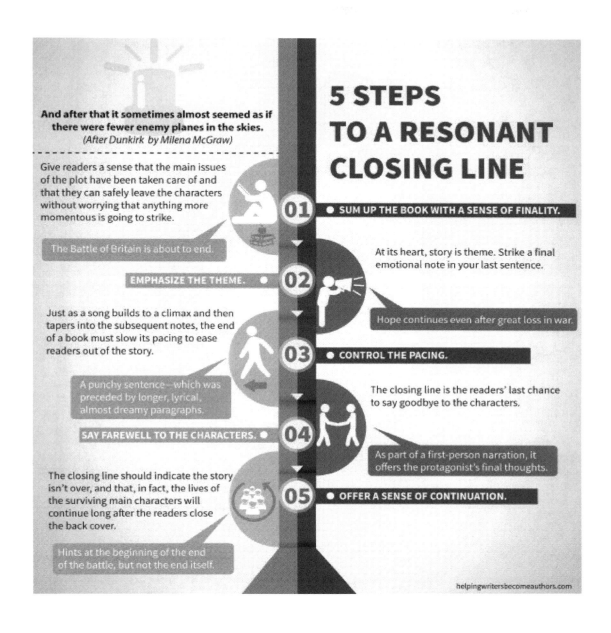

And after that it sometimes almost seemed as if there were fewer enemy planes in the skies.
(After Dunkirk by Milena McGraw)

Give readers a sense that the main issues of the plot have been taken care of and that they can safely leave the characters without worrying that anything more momentous is going to strike.

The Battle of Britain is about to end.

Just as a song builds to a climax and then tapers into the subsequent notes, the end of a book must slow its pacing to ease readers out of the story.

A punchy sentence—which was preceded by longer, lyrical, almost dreamy paragraphs.

The closing line should indicate the story isn't over, and that, in fact, the lives of the surviving main characters will continue long after the readers close the back cover.

Hints at the beginning of the end of the battle, but not the end itself.

5 STEPS TO A RESONANT CLOSING LINE

01 ● SUM UP THE BOOK WITH A SENSE OF FINALITY.

At its heart, story is theme. Strike a final emotional note in your last sentence.

EMPHASIZE THE THEME. ● **02**

Hope continues even after great loss in war.

03 ● CONTROL THE PACING.

The closing line is the readers' last chance to say goodbye to the characters.

SAY FAREWELL TO THE CHARACTERS. ● **04**

As part of a first-person narration, it offers the protagonist's final thoughts.

05 ● OFFER A SENSE OF CONTINUATION.

helpingwritersbecomeauthors.com

CREATIVE EXERCISE:

What books or movies have left you with a sustained feeling of satisfaction? Study their Resolution scenes and take note of the elements that evoked your emotional response. Can you replicate these techniques in your own Resolution?

SOMETHING TO THINK ABOUT:

1. Does your Resolution take place directly after the Climax? Is it the last scene(s) in the book?
2. How have you tied off all the prominent loose ends?
3. How have you avoided making your ending too perfect?
4. Does your Resolution offer readers a sense of continuation by hinting at the lives the characters will lead after readers have closed the back cover?
5. Does your Resolution give readers a concrete example of how the character's journey has changed him?
6. What emotional note does your Resolution strike? Does it resonate with the tone of the book as a whole (funny, romantic, melancholy, etc.)? Will it leave readers satisfied?

RESOURCES:

- "Elements of a Good Ending," Joe Moore, helpingwritersbecome authors.com/SYNW-Moore
- "The Characteristic Moment Belongs at the End of Your Book Too," K.M. Weiland, helpingwritersbecomeauthors.com/2013/10/characteristic-moment-belongs-end-book
- "Are the Loose Ends in Your Story *Too* Loose?" K.M. Weiland, helping writersbecomeauthors.com/2014/03/loose-ends-in-your-story
- "How Properly Structured Beginnings and Endings Hold Your Book Together," K.M. Weiland, helpingwritersbecomeauthors.com/2013/08/ properly-structured-beginnings-endings-hold-book-together
- "It's the End of the Book as We Know It," Krista Phillips, helpingwriters becomeauthors.com/SYNW-Phillips

PART 2:
STRUCTURING YOUR SCENES

10
SCENES

EVERY SCENE WITHIN your story has two halves: the scene (in which characters are acting) and the sequel (in which characters are reacting). These two mighty little pistons power the entirety of your story. We can further break these two halves down into three steps apiece (we'll take a look at the three parts of the sequel in the next chapter). Broken down into three pieces, the scene looks like this:

The Goal: Every scene begins with your character wanting something. The scene goal will always be a reflection or a result of the overall story goal. Your character wants to defeat the evil overlord or win the fair maiden's hand. To get there, he will have to enact a series of smaller goals. These goals will form the impetus for every scene. Identify your character's goal early in each scene to give its narrative focus and dynamism.

The Conflict: If your character were allowed to traipse right through your story, accomplishing his every goal, your plot would be over almost as quickly as it began. This is where conflict comes into play. Scene conflict takes the form of anything that prevents your character from achieving his scene goal. This might be a fistfight, or it might be a flat tire. Conflict is the meat of your scene. After you've set up the goal, the majority of your scene will focus on whatever it is that's keeping your character from getting what he wants.

The Outcome (or Disaster): Your scene will end with a decided outcome. Either your character overcomes the conflict to get what he wants, or, more likely, he fails either partly or wholly—and the scene ends in disaster. Every scene must push your character sideways instead of allowing him to advance uninhibited in a straight line to his main goal.

OPTIONS FOR GOALS IN A SCENE

THE POSSIBILITIES FOR scene goals are endless and very specific to your story. Your character can want anything in any given scene. But within that universe of options, you must narrow down the desires expressed in your scene to those that will drive the plot. Wanting to buy pink carnations for Mother's Day is a worthy goal, but if your character's mother is a nonexistent player in your story of a nuclear war, it's not going to belong in your story—and certainly not as a scene goal.

Scene goals are the dominoes in your story's plot. Each goal is a step forward in your story. One goal leads to a result that prompts a new goal and on and on. They knock into each other, one domino after another. If they *don't*—if one goal is out of place in the overall story—the line of dominoes will stop and the story will falter.

Refine your scene goals by asking the following questions.

(For more about scene goals, see pages 193-200 in *Structuring Your Novel*.)

Which of the following does your protagonist want in this scene?

☐ Something concrete (an object, a person, etc.).

What? _____.

☐ Something incorporeal (admiration, information, etc.).

What? _____.

☐ Escape from something physical (imprisonment, pain, etc.).

What? _____.

☐ Escape from something mental (worry, suspicion, fear, etc.).

What? _____.

☐ Escape from something emotional (grief, depression, etc.).

What? _____.

☐ Other.

What? _____.

Which of the following methods does your protagonist use to attempt to gain what he wants in this scene?

☐ Seeks information.

    How? _____.

☐ Hides information.

    How? _____.

☐ Hides self.

    How? _____.

☐ Hides someone else.

    How? _____.

☐ Confronts or attacks someone else.

    How? _____.

☐ Repairs or destroys physical objects.

    How? _____.

☐ Other.

    How? _____.

If applicable, ask yourself what goal your antagonist has in this scene that causes him to oppose the protagonist's goal.

Which of the following does your antagonist want in this scene?

☐ Something concrete (an object, a person, etc.).

    What? _____.

□ Something incorporeal (admiration, information, etc.).

What? _____.

□ Escape from something physical (imprisonment, pain, etc.).

What? _____.

□ Escape from something mental (worry, suspicion, fear, etc.).

What? _____.

□ Escape from something emotional (grief, depression, etc.).

What? _____.

□ Other.

What? _____.

Which of the following methods does your antagonist use to attempt to gain what he wants in this scene?

□ Seeks information.

How? _____.

□ Hides information.

How? _____.

□ Hides self.

How? _____.

□ Hides someone else.

How? _____.

☐ Confronts or attacks someone else.

How? _____.

☐ Repairs or destroys physical objects.

How? _____.

☐ Other.

How? _____.

Once you've identified your scene's goal, stop and ask yourself the following questions:

How does the protagonist's goal make sense within the overall plot? _____

_____.

How is the goal inherent to the overall plot? _____

_____.

How will the goal's complication/resolution lead to a new goal/conflict/disaster?

_____

_____.

If the goal is mental or emotional (e.g., be happy today), what is its physical

manifestation (e.g., smile at everyone)? _____

_____.

How does the success or failure of the goal directly affect the scene narrator? _____

_____.

OPTIONS FOR CONFLICT IN A SCENE

CONFLICT IS WHAT story is all about. Without it, the character would achieve his goal in minutes, all the loose ends would be tied off, and the story would be happily ever over. Conflict keeps your story moving forward. When the character's initial goal is stymied by conflict, it causes him to react with a new goal, which is stymied by further conflict, which causes him to again modify his goal—and on and on, until *finally* he reaches the goal and the story ends.

Don't be afraid of socking it to your characters. Without conflict and its associated suffering, characters have no reason to exist. Use the following questions to analyze your scenes to ensure each one erects obstacles between your character and his goal.

(For more on scene conflict, see pages 203-213 in *Structuring Your Novel*.)

Which of the following obstacles comes between your protagonist and what he wants in this scene?

☐ Direct opposition (another character, weather, etc., which interferes with and prevents the protagonist from achieving his goal).

What? _____.

☐ Inner opposition (the character learns something that changes his mind about his goal).

What? _____.

☐ Circumstantial difficulties (no flour to bake a cake, no partners to dance with, etc.).

What? _____.

☐ Active conflict (argument, fistfight, etc.).

What? _____.

☐ Passive conflict (being ignored, being kept in the dark, being avoided, etc.).

What? _____.

☐ Other.

What? _____.

How does this scene's obstacle manifest?

☐ Physical altercation.

How? _____.

☐ Verbal altercation.

How? _____.

☐ Physical obstacle (weather, roadblock, personal injury, etc.).

How? _____.

☐ Mental obstacle (fear, amnesia, etc.).

How? _____.

☐ Physical lack (no flour to bake a cake).

How? _____.

☐ Mental lack (no information).

How? _____.

☐ Passive aggression (intentional or unintentional).

How? _____.

☐ Indirect interference (long-distance or unintentional opposition by another character).

How? _____.

☐ Other.

How? _____.

Once you've identified your scene's conflict, ask yourself the following questions:

Why does the opposition to the character's goal *matter* to him? _____

_____.

How does the conflict evolve organically from the goal? _____

_____.

Why is the opposition's motivation logical within the overall story? _____

_____.

How does the conflict lead to a logical outcome (resolution or disaster) for the scene?

_____.

How does the conflict directly interfere with or threaten the protagonist's goal?

_____.

OPTIONS FOR DISASTERS IN A SCENE

T HE FINAL PART in the three-part structure of your scene is the outcome. The first two parts of the scene (the goal and the conflict) asked a specific question; the outcome will answer that question.

At the end of every single scene, search for a way to thwart your character's hopes. This does not, however, mean he should never gain ground toward achieving his goal. He can achieve part of his goal while still experiencing setbacks.

Sometimes, in order to advance the plot, your disasters are going to have to be incomplete. The *partial obstruction of goal* and the *hollow victory* are two examples. These "Yes, but!" disasters occur when your character gets a qualified or even total "yes" in answer to the scene question. He fulfills his scene goal, *but* there are complications.

The point is to keep the pressure on and never let up. The scene disaster pushes the character sideways, *away* from achieving his main goal, while pushing him unwittingly *toward* the thing he really needs (the final confrontation with the antagonistic force).

Answer the following questions about your scene disaster.

(For more on scene disasters, see pages 217-222 in *Structuring Your Novel*.)

Which of the following "disasters" ends your scene?

☐ Direct obstruction of the goal (e.g., the character wants info the antagonist refuses).

What? _____.

☐ Indirect obstruction of the goal (e.g., the character is sidetracked).

What? _____.

☐ Partial obstruction of the goal (e.g., the character gets only part of what he needs).

What? _____.

☐ Hollow victory (e.g., the character gets his want but it's destructive).

What? _____.

☐ Other.

What? _____.

How does this scene's disaster specifically manifest?

☐ Death.

How? _____.

☐ Physical injury.

How? _____.

☐ Emotional injury.

How? _____.

☐ Discovery of complicating information.

How? _____.

☐ Personal mistake.

How? _____.

☐ Threat to personal safety.

How? _____.

☐ Danger to someone else.

How? _____.

☐ Other.

How? _____.

Once you've identified your scene's disaster, stop and ask yourself the following questions:

How does your disaster answer the scene question, as posed by the scene goal?

_____

_____ .

How is your disaster integral to the scene (i.e., is the disaster a direct culmination

of the scene conflict)? _____

_____ .

Is your disaster disastrous enough? _____ .

Does your disaster avoid melodrama? _____ .

If your character partially or totally reaches his scene goal, what "yes, but!" disaster

is waiting to slow him down? _____

_____ .

What new goal will your disaster prompt from the character? _____

_____ .

CREATIVE EXERCISE:

What's the weather in your most important scenes? Does it reinforce or contrast the tone and thematic underpinnings of the scenes' events? Could you bolster any of these scenes by altering the weather?

SOMETHING TO THINK ABOUT:

1. What emotion or mindset does the protagonist have at the beginning of the scene?
2. What emotion or mindset does he have at the end of the scene?
3. How has the character's emotion evolved over the course of the scene?
4. What is the *primary* emotion in this scene?
5. Do the primary emotions vary from scene to scene to avoid repetition and to gain thematic depth?

RESOURCES:

- "Does Your Character Lack Purpose?" K.M. Weiland, helpingwriters becomeauthors.com/2012/09/writing-mistakes-17-character-purpose
- "Make Every Scene Matter," K.M. Weiland, helpingwritersbecome authors.com/2010/03/make-every-scene-matter
- "Scenes: The Building Blocks of Your Story," Justine Schofield, helpingwritersbecomeauthors.com/2012/08/scenes-building-blocks-of-your-story
- "Episodic Storytelling? Here's Why," K.M. Weiland, helpingwritersbecome authors.com/2013/02/episodic-storytelling-heres-why
- "Use Triangles to Help Your Readers Get the Point," Shanan, helping writers becomeauthors.com/SYNW-Shanan

THE EMOTIONAL PROGRESSION OF SCENE AND SEQUEL

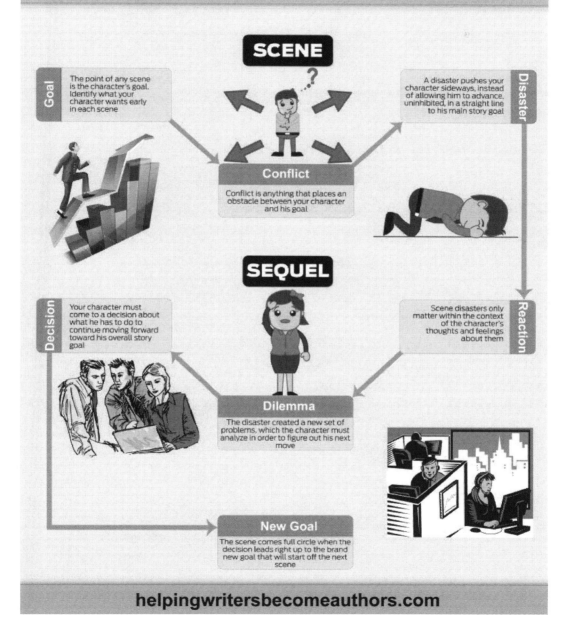

SCENE

Goal
The point of any scene is the character's goal. Identify what your character wants early in each scene

Disaster
A disaster pushes your character sideways, instead of allowing him to advance, uninhibited, in a straight line to his main story goal

Conflict
Conflict is anything that places an obstacle between your character and his goal

SEQUEL

Decision
Your character must come to a decision about what he has to do to continue moving forward toward his overall story goal

Reaction
Scene disasters only matter within the context of the character's thoughts and feelings about them

Dilemma
The disaster created a new set of problems, which the character must analyze in order to figure out his next move

New Goal
The scene comes full circle when the decision leads right up to the brand new goal that will start off the next scene

helpingwritersbecomeauthors.com

11
SEQUELS

ALTHOUGH THE SEQUEL possesses three basic and unavoidable parts, just like the scene, it is much more flexible in execution. The three parts may take place within a single sentence—or be stretched out over many chapters. Sometimes one or the other of the parts may be implied; sometimes they may appear to be intermixed with the pieces of the scene. These three parts are:

The Reaction: This is where the character reacts to what's just happened in the disaster at the end of the previous scene. This is an extremely important section. Not only does it allow a little "downtime" in between action set pieces, it also bolsters readers' suspension of disbelief by proving that your character is a thinking, reacting human being. Scene disasters only matter in the context of the character's thoughts and feelings about them.

The Dilemma: Once you've recorded your character's initial emotional reaction to the disaster, you have to allow his intellect to take over. The disaster will have presented him with a new dilemma. How will he move forward after this recent setback and its complications? The dilemma is where your character puts on his thinking cap and figures out his next move. This might be a lengthy section in which he ponders many options, or it might be just a quick sentence if the answer to his dilemma is obvious.

The Decision: The sequel (and the scene as a whole) ends when your character caps his dilemma with a decision. He figures out what he has to do to continue moving forward toward his overall story goal. This brings the scene as a whole full circle and leads right up to the brand new goal that will start off the next scene.

Once you understand the six factors needed to create solid scenes and sequels, you will have the building blocks you need to assemble your story from the ground up. Put one solid scene upon another—and before you know it, you'll have an entire story.

OPTIONS FOR REACTIONS IN A SEQUEL

A S SOON AS your previous scene's disaster hits, your character is going to experience an immediate and instinctive emotional reaction. Authors who lack a complete understanding of the scene/sequel structure sometimes worry their sequels won't contain enough action or conflict to keep readers' attention. But this is far from the case. Readers love action (whatever its manifestation), and authors can't create a story without it. But without character reactions, all that juicy action will lack context and, as a result, *meaning*.

Answer the following questions to identify and elaborate upon your character's reaction in the sequel.

(For more information on sequel reactions, see pages 233-238 in *Structuring Your Novel*.)

With which of the following emotions does your protagonist respond to the disaster in the previous scene?

☐ Elation.

How? _____.

☐ Fury.

How? _____.

☐ Anger.

How? _____.

☐ Confusion.

How? _____.

☐ Despair.

How? _____.

☐ Panic.

How? _____.

☐ Shame.

How? _____.

☐ Regret.

How? _____.

☐ Shock.

How? _____.

☐ Other.

How? _____.

Which of the following will you use to convey the above emotional reaction to your reader?

☐ Description.

How? _____.

☐ Internal narrative/monologue.

How? _____.

☐ Dramatization.

How? _____.

☐ Tone.

How? _____.

How does your character's reaction correlate to the preceding disaster? _____

_____.

Why does the character's reaction make sense in context with the preceding disaster?

_____.

Why is the character's reaction logical for his personality? _____

_____.

How much time, in the story, will you need to appropriately portray the reaction?

_____.

Can you illustrate the reaction more powerfully through narrative, description, action,

or dialogue? _____

_____.

How can you clarify the character's reaction to the disaster without unnecessarily

rehashing information readers are already familiar with? _____

_____.

OPTIONS FOR DILEMMAS IN A SEQUEL

THE DILEMMA IS composed of three different phases:

Review: The protagonist will look back on the disaster and consider the missteps that *allowed* it to happen. This phase is often intertwined with the preceding reaction section. Its length will largely depend on its proximity to the disaster and the pacing.

Analyze: Now that your character has progressed past his initial emotional reaction, he will have to start considering the specifics of his problem. The dilemma will always present a question, the gist of which is, "How do I get out of this mess?"

Plan: Once your character has sufficiently analyzed the problem, he will move into the planning phase—which will then segue right into the next section of the sequel: the decision (which we'll discuss in the next segment).

Plan your scene's dilemma using the following questions.

(For more information on sequel dilemmas, see pages 241-245 of *Structuring Your Novel*.)

How will your protagonist work through each phase of the dilemma stage?

Review: _____

_____

_____.

Is it actually necessary to review the disaster in order to remind readers what happened? ☐ Yes ☐ No

Analyze: _____

_____

_____.

State your protagonist's problem as a specific question (see examples on next page):

_____.

EXAMPLES:

- **How will he get out of this snake pit?**
- **How will she get Joey to forgive her for lying to him?**
- **How can he find money to buy groceries?**

Plan: _____

_____

_____.

How much depth will you need to go into in order to properly flesh out your sequel dilemma?

- ☐ Indicate the dilemma implicitly (e.g., by allowing the reader to presume the dilemma based on the previous disaster).

- ☐ Indicate the dilemma explicitly by summarizing/telling it (e.g., "Marti had to figure out how to get some groceries before they all starved").

- ☐ Indicate the dilemma explicitly by dramatizing/showing it (e.g., Marti's stomach growls).

How is the dilemma influenced by the disaster at the end of the previous scene?

_____.

How have you made sure the dilemma is clear to readers? _____

_____.

Why does the amount of time you spend on the dilemma match its importance

within the plot?_____.

If you've chosen to include a review section of the preceding scene, how does it

avoid repetition? _____.

OPTIONS FOR DECISIONS IN A SEQUEL

PERHAPS THE MOST instinctive of all the scene/sequel building blocks is the decision. This third and final piece of the sequel grows out of the character's dilemma and leads right into the next scene's goal. The decision is the little cattle prod on your story's backside that keeps it moving forward. Conceivably, your character could sit around contemplating his dilemmas for the rest of his life. But good stories require forward motion, and the only way out of a dilemma is to make a decision—whether it's right or wrong.

As always, the key to a good decision is making sure it is a direct result of the previous dilemma. A random, unrelated decision may well keep the plot moving, but not in the straight line your readers want. If your character's dilemma is about what to make for dinner, his decision needs to be to make filet mignon and lyonnaise potatoes—not to run down to the hospital and donate blood.

Answer the following questions about your sequel's decision.

(For more on sequel decisions, see pages 249-254 in *Structuring Your Novel*.)

What action will your character decide to take? _____

_____.

How is your decision an organic result of your dilemma? _____

_____.

How will your decision lead into a strong goal? _____

_____.

If your dilemma is a long-term problem, how have you narrowed the decision down

to the first logical step in solving that problem? _____

_____.

What new complications will arise from your character's decision? _____

_____.

If your character decides *not* to take action, how is this non-action a logical and

important step that advances the conflict? _____

_____.

Is your character's decision important enough to explicitly state it in the sequel?

_____

_____.

    If you've stated the decision outright, how have you kept it from being repetitious

in light of either the previous dilemma or the following goal? _____

_____.

CREATIVE EXERCISE:

With what emotion does your character react to a recent disaster? Write an alternative sequel in which he responds to the disaster with exactly the opposite emotion. How does the story change for the better or worse?

SOMETHING TO THINK ABOUT:

1. What emotion or mindset does your protagonist have at the beginning of the sequel?
2. How does this emotion evolve over the course of the sequel?
3. What prominent emotion or mindset does the protagonist have at the end of the sequel?
4. What primary emotion defines this sequel?
5. How does this primary emotion vary from that in other sequels throughout the story?

RESOURCES:

- "How to Use Foreshadowing to Jazz Up Slow Scenes," K.M. Weiland, helpingwritersbecomeauthors.com/2012/08/how-to-use-foreshadowing-to-jazz-up
- "How to Cut the Filler and Tighten Your Book," Laura Carlson, helpingwriters becomeauthors.com/2012/12/how-to-cut-filler-and-tighten-your-book
- "Warning Signs! Your Character Is Acting Out of Character," K.M. Weiland, helpingwritersbecomeauthors.com/2014/01/out-of-character
- "5 Ways You're Preventing Readers From Suspending Their Disbelief," K.M. Weiland, helpingwritersbecomeauthors.com/2012/08/5-ways-youre-preventing-readers-from

CONCLUSION

L ET ME TELL you the story of three novels.

One I wrote before I had any notion of story structure. One I wrote *as* I was discovering structure. And one I wrote years later.

The first two books share a similar fate, and that fate can pretty much be summed up with one word: revision. Lots and lots of revision. I loved these stories. I poured my heart and soul into them. But they didn't love me back. They were like wild birds, caged on the page, but fighting back at every turn.

My subconscious story sense (my gut instinct) told me loudly and clearly that something major was wrong with both of these stories. So I'd tweak this and tweak that. But I just couldn't get them to work. I didn't yet have the conscious knowledge of story structure to be able to understand *where* the stories were going wrong.

So I'd tweak, edit, and rewrite yet again.

The result was exhausting. While writing the first of these books, I became so overwhelmed I found myself wondering if writing would ever again be *fun*. While writing the second book, I came to a point when I finally had to admit the story wasn't working and I didn't know how to fix it. It became the only novel I ever quit on after completing the entire draft.

But in between that rocky education period of Book Two and that marvelous new understanding of story structure in Book Three, something changed.

That third book was one of the best writing experiences I've ever had. It was the fastest outline, fastest first draft, and fastest revision process I've ever experienced. Partly, that was probably due to the story itself. Every book, after all, is its own unique journey. But, *mostly*, that was due to the fact that, for the first time ever, I actually understood how to piece together a story that *worked*.

And, just like that, writing was fun again. Boy howdy, was it fun again.

Structure should never be about forcing our stories into a box. Structure is about creating a framework to support ideas—and then letting our imaginations fly free.

I hope you find this workbook and the structural principles it presents to be the key to your best stories yet. Grab a pen, start writing, and unlock the possibilities!

K.M. Weiland
November 2014

Note From the Author: Thanks so much for reading! I hope you've enjoyed our exploration of story structure and have closed this workbook prepared to write an incredible story. Did you know reviews sell books? If the *Structuring Your Novel Workbook* was helpful to you, would you consider rating and reviewing it on Amazon.com? Thank you and happy writing!

Want more writing tips? Join my mailing list at helpingwritersbecomeauthors.com/structuring-your-novel-signup to receive my monthly e-letter, full of writing tips, answered questions, creativity jump-starters, inspirational quotes, updates about new books and workshops, and the free e-book *Crafting Unforgettable Characters*.

Join the discussion: #StructuringYourNovel

Acknowledgments

I LOVE WRITING the acknowledgments page, because it means sitting down and thinking about all the lovely and selfless people who have spent time and energy helping me with the sometimes monumental task of creating a book. In the production of every book, there are always a handful of very specific people who had a direct influence upon the project. For this book, those people include (in no particular order):

My friends and beta readers, who astonish me with their generosity every time I ask for yet another favor:

Braden Russell—who always makes me think and, even better, laugh.

Steve Mathisen—who is just about as sweet as his Pooh avatar.

Lorna G. Poston—whom I know I can always depend on for honesty and encouragement.

Marie-Gaye Barton—whose enthusiasm is amazing.

I also have to extend a huge thank you to Jim Berning, who gets all the credit for coming up with the workbook idea in the first place.

And finally, thanks, as always, to my family for their support and encouragement—and especially to my #1 fan, sister, and assistant Amy.

ABOUT THE AUTHOR

K.M. WEILAND LIVES in make-believe worlds, talks to imaginary friends, and survives primarily on chocolate truffles and espresso. She is the IPPY and NIEA Award-winning and internationally published author of the Amazon bestsellers *Outlining Your Novel* and *Structuring Your Novel*, as well as *Jane Eyre: The Writer's Digest Annotated Classic*, the western *A Man Called Outlaw*, the medieval epic *Behold the Dawn*, and the portal fantasy *Dreamlander*. When she's not making things up, she's busy mentoring other authors through her award-winning blog HelpingWritersBecomeAuthors.com. She makes her home in western Nebraska. Visit her at KMWeiland.com or follow her on Twitter (@KMWeiland) to participate in her Writing Question of the Day (#WQOTD). You can email her at km.weiland@ymail.com.

FURTHER RESOURCES

The Positive Trait Thesaurus:
A Writer's Guide to Character Attributes
by Angela Ackerman & Becca Puglisi

Brimming with ideas to help authors develop one-of-a-kind, dynamic characters through a large selection of positive attributes that will help them overcome any obstacle.

http://amzn.to/1wD8Hik

Write Your Novel From the Middle:
A New Approach for Plotters, Pantsers and Everyone in Between
by James Scott Bell

A truly original concept about the most important moment in your novel, the "mirror moment," and how it can be used to create unforgettable fiction.

http://amzn.to/1oXk4jX

Learn How to Make Your First Draft Easy!

The *Outlining Your Novel Workbook* will show you how to:

- Create your own personalized outlining process
- Brainstorm premise and plot ideas
- Discover your characters
- Choose and create the right settings0
- Organize your scenes
- And so much more!

www.helpingwritersbecomeauthors.com

Made in the USA
San Bernardino, CA
17 March 2016